BE HAPPY MORE OFTEN

QUICKLY INCREASE YOUR HAPPINESS AND
POSITIVITY EVEN WHEN TIMES ARE TOUGH!
WITH 25 EXERCISES FOR LEADING A HAPPIER
LIFE!

A-J PATERSON

miniteachingmedia▸

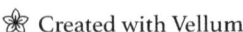

To my friends and family, especially my partner and children, for making my world a fun, encouraging and loving place to be.

Each positive humanitarian born to the world gives hope for others facing the difficulties and challenges of life.

The 1st law of thermodynamics:

    Energy cannot be created nor destroyed, only transformed.

INTRODUCTION

Have you ever met someone new or known someone who radiated a feeling of comfort or ease when you were in their presence? There was just something about them that made you feel safe and grounded. You sensed their optimistic strength, non-judgement of the world around them and their overall happiness and acceptance of life. They may not have appeared happy physically, after all, not many of us match the expected physical image of happiness that we see in the media; they were just a happy soul.

Contrary to popular culture, happiness is not exclusive to those who present as the life and soul of the party like a blazing ball of energy, dominating the space and leading the conversation. Many happy people exude a gentle energy that makes all those around them feel comfortable, even if they say little or appear shy. Their energy glows, in a warm and welcoming aura. It's as if they live some secret that few others have discovered, and they somehow manage to sustain it through thick and thin times.

There are simple philosophies and actions behind living a positive and happy life, whether you learn them consciously now by reading my book or are one of the lucky few to have unconsciously learned them for yourself.

Once you have finished my book, you too will know how to live, and inspire others to live, in happiness.

In many of my presentations, when I have asked the audience, "Out of all your feelings, which feeling would like to experience the most of in life?" the response has overwhelmingly been "More happiness."

When we then go on to brainstorm all of the perceived obstacles to happiness, these are the main thoughts that recur:

- "Life is difficult, challenging, or just plain too hard to be happy."
- "No-one has taught me how to be happy."
- "Happy people appear false; how can they be happy about things all the time?"
- "Life is full of disappointment."
- "Some people are just born lucky, fortunate or successful."
- "Happiness comes with money."
- "I can't be happy until I have ...."
- "I can't be properly happy until I've met the right person."

Although many of these thoughts can challenge us all at times, let's keep things in perspective:

- Life can be hard as there are ups and downs and we are not on this planet forever, nor are our nearest and dearest.
- "Happiness" is not a subject taught at school; however, wellbeing and mental health is beginning to become a priority in both schools and the workplace.
- People who always appear happy may seem suspect to those 'realists' who aren't, but does that mean that you can't be happy most of the time?
- Some people may have had things come to them easily but that does not necessarily mean that happiness comes from luck, you may not have seen the hard work behind their 'success.'

- Relying on having a partner or partners in life in order for you to feel better is dependency, and you need to be responsible for your own feelings first. There are many unhappy people who have a partner or partners, and many happy people who are single.

We are not mind-readers and we often mistakenly only judge what we observe about others as fact. Feelings can often be unobservable, as are the thoughts behind them. Some people can present a very happy and positive personality to the outside world but are actually experiencing inner turmoil in their personal thinking. This is why we should not assume that someone is happy by appearance alone. As you read further, you will experience more happiness through understanding how your feelings and thoughts work, learn how to take control of what you actually can, and let go of what you simply can't.

I spent many years in search of happiness, joining groups, studying cognitive-behavioural therapy, hypnosis and neuro-linguistic programming. In my quest for happiness, I have experienced re-birthing, shouted out my Walt Whitman barbaric 'Yawp!' 'Dead Poet Society' style, worked on my Chi and explored Stoicism and other philosophies. I have met with world-famous self-help gurus, mindfulness practitioners and motivational coaches. Many of them do lead happy and positive lifestyles and some don't practice what they preach at all. In this book, I present you with the essence of what really works from all of my learnings and with the same information I have helped so many others with to change their lives for the better.

The most profound Scientists and Philosophers teach that if someone else can do or experience something, the odds are that you most likely can reproduce the same or similar results. From Socrates to Newton, we have been taught that we can observe, test, rationalise, theorise, predict, and ask questions in order to form our own conclusions. Many of us simply don't bother or choose to do so from a negative bias. Negative people who don't commit to apply things in the real world, instead, walk through life making quick judgements without any substantial evidence at all. If you believe that people simply can't be mostly happy in life, then maybe you have not met the many of us who are. Some "realists" have suspiciously dismissed consistent happiness as "unrealistic" or "Out of touch with reality." They have not learned how to live life happily more often.

The Stoics of Ancient Greece and Rome believed that we have no control of anything except our own attitudes to life and the state of our feelings and reactions. Happiness is a feeling that comes from a thought and is a state we can choose to experience.

Your personal values guide you in life, they shape your beliefs, your thoughts and your feelings. You can choose to be proactive, happy, and positive, with a focus on seeing the brighter side of events, just as you can choose to be cautious, suspicious and cynical about life and others.

Which approach serves your life better?

Do you ever say?

"Why me?" or feel that the "The grass is always greener on the other side of the fence."

Or do you pep yourself up in an encouraging way?

"OK, let's get on and sort this out." Or

"What positive lesson can I learn from this event?"

The way that we view the world is a personal choice. It is the shade of glasses we wear to filter our world, whether they be dark or rose-tinted.

This book is about how happy people face the world and even the most challenging and difficult events that leave others regularly upset, frustrated and dysfunctional. Most importantly, this book teaches the beliefs and actions for you to do the same.

1

PREPARING FOR A POSITIVE CHANGE
CHANGE NOTHING AND NOTHING WILL CHANGE

Before we begin our journey to experiencing more happiness, the following preparation is worth your attention before you proceed. This short chapter is important to help clarify what happiness is, and then clarify what you consider are your own unique obstacles to feeling happy. It is an exercise that requires some deep thinking and your ability to be objective as well. Firstly, let's understand the four different states of happiness.

1. Happiness through your senses: Short-term happiness is the result of appreciating "simple pleasures". Simple pleasures are as the name implies, simple actions we take that result in our pleasure, which we enjoy in that moment of time. Eating, romance, a chat with a friend, an enjoyable film, a concert, theatre, an art gallery, a great coffee or tea, enjoying a hobby, going for a run, your favourite music, a motivational podcast, sex, and feeling cosy at home are all examples of simple pleasures. The feeling of happiness is instant and will last as long as the experience. Building simple pleasures throughout the day will help to sustain our feeling of happiness.

2. Happiness through your thinking: Knowing you have choice and exercising it gives us a sense of control, freedom and happiness. Your well-being is effected by your thoughts and reactions to the world around you. If you react in a negative way to events, you will focus on all the reasons you are not happy. If you have positive beliefs and choose constructive reactions, you will see the brighter side of situations and you will react in a proactive way that improves your situation.

3. Happiness through a higher meaning: Having a strong sense of the meaning of your life and exercising your potential to live up to that meaning will bring you happiness. You have recognised and fulfilled your creative talents to the point of self-actualisation. Simply put, you have achieved your highest dreams.

4. Happiness through Acceptance: Transcending all these states is a "meta" state of happiness. In Greek, "meta" means above or beyond. To achieve a meta state of happiness your thinking is raised above your physical and mental condition as a human being and you accept all around you as "It just is." You will have a better acceptance of what it is to be human and choose to experience happiness in most situations.

Happy Language

In this book you will read the word "happiness" and "positive" many times over. This is my way of keeping a clear thread rather than using different words with a similar meaning. It is comforting to know that there are many other words to describe happiness and a large number of ways we can experience this state. Following is a list of varying "happy" states of differing degrees:

- Blessed

- Blissful
- Blithe
- Captivated
- Cheerful
- Chipper
- Chirpy
- Congenial
- Content
- Convivial
- Delighted
- Ecstatic
- Elated
- Exultant
- Glad
- Gleeful
- Gratified
- High
- Intoxicated
- Jolly
- Joyful
- Joyous
- Jubilant
- Light
- Lively
- Merry
- Mirthful
- On cloud nine
- Overjoyed
- Peaceful
- Peppy
- Perky
- Playful
- Pleasant
- Pleased
- Sparkling

- Sunny
- Thrilled
- Tickled pink
- Up
- Upbeat
- Walking on air

The Events in Our Life

Life is composed of many experiences and some appear deeply tragic and unjust, whether they be natural disasters, or human-caused disasters. How you react and adapt in even the most trying circumstances is dependent on your beliefs and mindset. Many people believe that our existence is not limited to what we experience on earth and others relate more to the natural circle of life and the nature of the Universe. Many others walk around in denial and do not accept the reality of our life or avoid giving it thought. Whatever your personal belief and take on your existence, you will have a different scale of reaction to even the smallest of setbacks.

Let's take the most difficult situation for most people, death and leaving our life on earth. Like us all, having had people very close to me who have died after an illness or an accident over a short and long period of time, I have seen different reactions to the end of life. One close friend showed optimism and gratefulness for his family right until his death even though he was relatively young; whereas a grandparent of mine who had lived a long life was extremely unhappy and sorrowful and only resigned to accept their death near the very end; whilst another friend very dear to me went through a mix of feelings: Anger, depression, sorrow, then acceptance and peace at the moment they passed.

Why have I presented you with such a morbid example of unhappiness? It's insightful to know your most extreme unhappy event and rank it as a 10/10 in terms of its perceived impact on your happiness and optimism for life. Though death isn't everyone's idea of the worst thing that would impact upon their happiness, it is highly common.

From this point you can then find a way of putting every other setback you worry about in perspective and assign it a rank out of 10, 1 being the lowest impact.

Exercise 1: Ranking your challenges to happiness

Rate out of 10 how events effect your happiness. Anything 8 or lower should be challenging but manageable through a positive mind frame, a happy outlook, and taking proactive actions to make things better.

For example, maybe a small cut would rate 1 out of 10 for the momentary pain it brings you.

Maybe a critical comment at work ranks around a 3 or 4.

Maybe not getting into the course of your first choice ranks around a 5 or 6.

Maybe that loss of a competition or examination you have practiced for ranks around a 7.

Perhaps a recent relationship break-up ranks around an 8.

Maybe the revelation of a serious illness of someone you love or yourself ranks around a 9.

Maybe the permanent loss of someone through death is a 10 in terms of how much your happiness will be affected.

Extreme impact on my happiness

10.

9.

8.

7.

6.

5.

4.

3.

2.

1.

Little impact on my happiness

.   .   .

NOW YOU HAVE A BETTER picture of yourself, would you like to be less sensitive in your reactions to each of these events?

Are there areas on your list where you would rather feel happier and more optimistic when they occur?

Ask yourself the following questions:

- In your view, aside from your own demise, what would have to happen for you never to be happy or positive again?
- Why do you feel that you could never be happy again after this?
- Would other people have the same response about this?
- If other people wouldn't have the same response as you, what would they be thinking, feeling or doing differently?

UNHAPPINESS MAINLY OCCURS THROUGH DISAPPOINTMENT, regret, fear, tragedy and emotional pain, such as heartache. We all bounce back differently to an event, or sometimes not at all. It depends on our reaction and outlook on the event. Know that most feelings pass and can pass even faster with a positive take on even the most difficult situation. Some people do not even believe their happiness ends after death and that they will even be happier when they pass from this world.

BEING HAPPY IS A PERSONAL JOURNEY. Keep reading to learn how to improve your reactions to disappointing experiences and create many more opportunities to be happy.

2

AN EXCUSE IS OF NO USE

DO WHAT YOU SAY YOU ARE GOING TO DO

M aking excuses and being irresponsible is the quickest route to discontent and unhappiness. Happy people consciously choose their path to more happy moments. You won't see them indulging in things that will bring them down, especially random external events and setbacks.

The necessity of taking risks

In life you take risks. From the moment you were born, you were learning, and learning fast. You learned to pull yourself along the floor, then get upon your knees and crawl, stand up using support, stand independently, and then you finally took your first steps. You made many mistakes and fell over, and sometimes cried. You also smiled, giggled and laughed as you independently tottered about the room.

Considering how you started your life and achieved amazing feats in your learning and physical abilities, why be fearful? If you now avoid mistakes and taking risks, and instead worry about the fairness of the external events of life of which you have no control, no wonder you may experience limited happiness.

When I was a teenager, I played a lot of soccer. One evening I played a match against a rival team and scored a few goals in what I felt was one of my best games. It had been raining and it was cold, and I probably pushed my performance a little too hard.

The very next day I fell ill. For a fortnight I felt like I had a continual flu and became fatigued to the point of not being able to get out of bed, and it wasn't improving. I needed a home visit from the Doctor as I was so debilitated. After a return of a blood test, the doctor came to the conclusion that I had glandular fever from contracting the Epstein-Barr virus. The only cure was time and rest.

After months of illness, my Doctor suggested I should start making the effort to get up with no excuses for feeling ill or tired, I had to push past the fatigue. I started by carefully rolling out of bed onto the floor and then crawling to the bathroom. I had to fight the fatigue each morning simply to take a shower. This effort to push past the fatigue helped me make a faster recovery. Eventually I returned to my beloved soccer after an 18 month absence.

The words from my Doctor that still ring in my ears and made all the difference were "No Excuses!"

No Excuses

Happiness is for the willing and the brave. If you continue to sit in front of the TV or live a life through social media without making the conscious effort to change, you are losing your chance to see beyond the limits of a media-shaped world. If you don't take charge of your choices, someone else will take charge of your choices for you, and the media is great for doing this without your conscious consent; after all, their intention is to influence you and make money at your expense.

It is time to stop labelling things in extremes like fair or unfair, good or bad, and right or wrong. The world is complicated and there are many shades of grey. Your greatest ability is to learn to be responsible for controlling your own feelings and how you react positively to external events. That is the very best you can do for yourself and others. When you've taken responsibility for your own beliefs and actions, you can begin to influence and inspire change around you. Though you cannot control the events of the world or the thoughts and actions of other people, you can certainly inspire others with your own positive thoughts and actions. As a happy person you want to act responsibly and proactively. If you present as a whiney, wimpy, disempowered, negative representation of yourself to the world, you just appear weak; you give in to the external events outside of your control.

Choosing a Side

How you perceive the world is exactly how you will experience it. You may see the beauty of a sunrise by choosing to get up early, or you may see the hassle of leaving the comfort of your bed, not bother, and miss out on an opportunity.

Through your choice of thinking positively or negatively, you will attract beauty in your life, or you will attract inaction and possible fear.

Positive choice takes responsibility, while negative choice is the action of blaming forces outside of yourself and behaving irresponsibly.

If you expect to do your best in that moment, your best will satisfy feeling good after having made the effort. If you expect to fail and fear being embarrassed in front of others, you will likely experience exactly that, having mentally set yourself up to for this eventuation.

To face your fears is to grow. It is a part of having your mind set on growing and improving. Your mistakes help you to learn and make a success of the oncoming next opportunity to apply what you have learnt.

You get what you project

Think of what you are responsible for:

- Your choice of job and career.
- Your choice of beliefs, whether they be positive or negative, ambitious or average, inspiring or lacklustre.
- Your choice of how you feel, even right now in this very moment.
- Your reactions to events and the actions you respond with.

You see, like attracts like. Fear attracts fearful events and optimism attracts positive events. Events sometimes just unfold with no personal involvement; however, it is your reaction to them in a fearful or optimistic state of mind that counts. A fearful state of mind will make your feelings about the experience worse, while a positive state of mind will open you up to more beneficial choices.

When you choose to change your deepest beliefs about the world, your life changes too. Once we make a decision to do something, the means to complete it are often revealed from our unconscious mind. The unconscious mind controls all those automated aspects of your life that you cannot handle consciously: the beating of your heart, breathing, and your background thoughts and actions. The unconscious also makes use of the creative part of our brain to find solutions to challenges and issues while you consciously get on with the things you need to do in your everyday life. You need to give your unconscious daydreaming more credit for the many problems solved when you don't even seem aware of anything going on.

Making the effort

Have you ever had a friend say to you something along the line of,

"Everything goes wrong in my life and it's just unfair! How come others have it so easy?"

Not the most proactive, nor responsible way to view events is it? Not much will improve for this person until they either start to do something with the positive strengths that they already have, or in the rarest of circumstances, that someone sorts it out for them.

In our world, we are rewarded for the efforts we make which

come from us alone in most situations. We are no longer children and friends and family have their own personal stuff going on to keep them busy. Of course, there is always someone out there to reach out to when you need help, support and advice, but you need to do the work with your own effort and persistence.

The unconscious mind is always sending us messages

The unconscious mind operates automatically behind our conscious, everyday thinking to protect our survival and wellbeing. It ensures that our physical and cognitive processes occur without fail, including the beating of our heart. The unconscious gives us protective warning signs in the form of emotional and physical pain, depending on the danger. If we are apathetic and don't take notice of these signals, doubts and negative thoughts about the situation may play out in our mind. Signals can be in the form of seeming to sabotage ourselves by eating badly or not eating at all, feeling anxious, angry or frustrated. These signals are to catch our attention and call us to take action and change our circumstances. When you notice these signals, ask:

- "How will this situation be in one year's time if I don't do anything about it now?"

Typically, worse!

Take a look at these common scenarios:

- You can't pay your bills from month to month and you begin to spiral into debt.
- You don't get that painful tooth checked and it becomes a root canal situation or has to be extracted.
- You don't show love to your partner, they become distant and they possibly find someone else who does reciprocate the love they need.

Consequences for negative choices

If you often ask, "Why me?" then you are acting powerlessly and need to take control of your life.

Maybe you practice habits that are hard to give up. Habits are common for most of us and the majority of them benefit our health and wellbeing. However, the few negative habits we practice are the behaviours we need to take responsibility for as they seem to occupy our thoughts and actions.

What are your positive habits?

What are your negative habits?

Maybe you have an addiction that has a psychological and/or physical hold on you and you feel dependent on it to temporarily feel good. Always seek professional psychological and medical help for addictions.

Do you have any addictions that you must satisfy frequently to feel some relief and comfort psychologically and physically?

Seeking comfort or escape in the form of habits and addictions such as procrastination, food, gaming, alcohol, drugs, gambling or any other form of destructive behaviour, will eventually put you in a very uncomfortable situation. They will catch up with you and there will be a price to pay bigger than the positive changes you could make right now by replacing these negative practices and choosing positive actions in their place.

Why irresponsible choices occur

Irresponsibility often leads to anger, frustration, unhappiness, and even criminality. Being angry at others is the biggest sign of irresponsibility. It shows that you have lost control of your actions and reactions and are now controlled by external events that you have no control over. You have given your power to someone or something outside of yourself and your reward is a negative feeling. You are saying that certain individuals or the world does not meet your rules and expectations of how things must be. You expect one thing to happen but unsurprisingly, something else happens instead.

You get into an argument with a friend. Why? Because they don't see things as you do. Well, you don't see things as they do either. Having a friend means you must expect and accept that you won't agree with everything they say, otherwise why have them as a friend? They are simply not you and you are not them.

Road rage is the result of anger to others for not following your rules or the "Official road laws." Unless you are a policeman, there is little that you can do to teach that person a lesson unless you are willing to report them or confront them at your own risk. Why escalate the situation with the possibility that more laws will be broken due to your upset. Instead, feel happy that you follow the rules and let professional law enforcement handle those if they are caught breaking them.

You get angry because someone makes you feel smaller than them by teasing or goading you; your femininity, masculinity, honour or reputation is at stake. Be happy knowing that you can be a strong and independent person and not let others upset you. You know deep inside who you really are, and you are also wise to their manipulation to wind you up and try and get a reaction. You choose not to play along with it. You act from awareness and maturity.

Your expectation that others should be nice, friendly, on-side or subordinate are wrong and will set you up for constant disappointment. Instead, look for the good in others and keep your own standards high and your expectations for others low. Most people don't think like you and you are not here to control their thoughts. There is no place in this world for "Thought Police."

Happy people have fewer expectations about others and external events, they react to what comes their way with positivity and learning, not defensiveness and threat.

Be Humble and Let Go of your Ego. Angry people feel they need their importance (ego) recognised by others and that they are right in the situation that has raised their emotions. They get angry when they don't get what they want as their expectations, realistic or not, have not been met.

Be mindful and accept reality as you cannot argue with it, you can only happily accept it and positively make use of it. If you try to forcibly change the world to the way you want it to be, you will find that others will rebel as they do not want their things changed to your way. Other people are just not you. There are extremes of opinions, beliefs and behaviours and so many shades of grey. Bad things happen in life and people do bad things. Good things happen in life and people do good things too. You cannot control this, but you can accept that any or all possibilities may happen and get on and reframe things in a positive light that will help yourself or possibly others in the future.

Exercise 2: Take an objective viewpoint

Make it a habit and practice to reflect on any challenging situation you have encountered in your day and imagine facing it in a positive way. Try the following approach:

1. Imagine seeing yourself in the challenging situation at a distance, not seeing the scene through your own eyes. This is called dissociation.
2. Imagine that instead of reacting in a negative way, you just listen and observe the other person/people and the event objectively without responding with any emotion. The important thing is to not react.
3. Imagine smiling internally or externally throughout the whole event as it plays out.
4. Imagine being mature and above the event and seeing it in perspective from a point of wisdom and experience. Watch the other person/people run out of emotional steam, or the event peter out into calmness.

"Dress your best" to encourage happiness

Reality will steamroll over anyone who defiantly stands in its way.

If you ever feel like you are stuck in a rut and not moving, here is a rule that I live by:

- "When you are at your worst, dress your best!"

I believe it to be an old saying, however I came across it when I read the biography of the classic Hollywood actor Errol Flynn, "My Wicked, Wicked Ways" (ghost-writer Earl Conrad).

You can take it literally and physically dress your best to lift yourself into a positive state, and you can take it figuratively and present your best even when you don't immediately feel it. It lines up with the saying, "Fake it until you make it" which relies on your habits changing for the better, by acting as if you are already experiencing the feeling you desire.

This is a very important practice to live by. Experience the desired feeling first, rather than as a reaction to an event that does not have a guaranteed outcome. You can change your feelings using your physiology to start. Stand tall and force a grin or a smile. Let that smile move into your eyes. You will notice a difference.

Let's see how else we can apply this saying.

I'm sure there have been times when you have said, "I hate my job!" If you are so unhappy with your job, start to "Dress your best." Give your best effort and attention, and you may find that after time your skills will improve, your reputation will rise, you may be offered a better role or responsibilities, or rewarded in another way. As a result, you may begin to feel a lot better about yourself and your job.

Like attracts like and if we focus on doing our best, opportunities will often appear when we are in a better, more positive state and also when we least expect them. When we feel badly about ourselves and negative about the situation we are in, things lose their shine and cheer and become worse.

When you feel positivity and happiness in one area of your life, happiness tends to spread across all areas of your life.

Emphasise what you have got, and you can expect to get even bigger opportunities.

Adapting to what we have more of in our lives

We always get used to what we have more of in life. As humans we quickly adapt to what surrounds us, whether good or bad. We become comfortable, even in the most trying of circumstances. It is in our nature to survive. If we are under significant threat, we will change in an instant to preserve our life.

The problem is that in order to adapt, we have to fit in. This means if we are around negative people, our actions can become negative in order to fit in. Criticising and blaming others for our life woes are what we will do if we are surrounded by peers doing the exact same thing. Abusing others becomes a norm if you are around abusive people. Lying, stealing and cheating will become the way to do things if that is how you learn to survive in your environment.

The great news is that we can also adapt and become comfortable with happy and positive thoughts and actions. The more we consciously practice being positive, the more second-nature it becomes. If you feel like your environment is negative, be the leader for change by not succumbing to negative peer pressure. You do not have to preach to anyone else, you just role-model positivity and happiness in your reactions to others and events. If you were to choose only positive and happy people as the friends you associate with, how would that change you?

You would likely value their positive perspective and how nothing daunts them. This will rub off on you as you experience how much happier you feel in their company.

You may live in a difficult environment but that does not mean you have to spend all your time there. Choose clubs, groups, or other environments where your chance of meeting better role-models increases or where you can practice being a better role-model your-self. You may make some positive new friends.

People who are pessimists will drain you, just like vampires need your blood to feed on. Negative people often need to affirm their misery by encouraging the misery of others. Their need is for you to feel just as bad as they do so that you have something in common. You don't want friends who feed upon you in negative ways, you want friends who energise you and you can energise them through a shared positive outlook.

Turn your challenges into proactive feedback and new opportunities

Use feedback to learn something more about your interests and capa-bilities and then use the results to improve your position. It may take you in a new exciting direction you were not even aware of. Always think that everything is feedback to help improve your under-standing of life and the positive actions you can make to contribute to our world.

A close friend of mine, Kate, was an amazingly talented dancer and singer in musical theatre shows and she had trained for many years to get there. When Kate began to get arthritis, while still in her early twenties, she was unable to continue dancing in the chorus due to the pain. With much work she began to work her way into small roles and then lead roles where there was less of a requirement to dance and an opportunity to utilise her singing talent. Kate became very successful until the taxing toll of singing show after show led to an operation to remove nodules on her vocal cords. This left Kate with a huskier voice and a shorter vocal range. As her chances in musical theatre were limited she reluctantly had to bring in income in another way. Many would just give up, but friends noticed that Kate's slightly husky voice was very attractive to listen to. Inspired by the comment, she went on to train in voiceover work and now is heard in many radio advertisements and has a daily DJ shift on a popular commercial radio. Kate turned her strengths into opportunities; her strength to entertain and her voice training. Kate now has a profession she loves even more than her musical theatre days.

One client I worked with in my personal practice, Aidan, was addicted to gambling through horse racing. Aidan quickly managed to lose his reputation and small fortune as a Barrister in the City of London within the space of a year. The more money he was paid, the higher the bets Aidan made, and although he managed a few big wins, he also accumulated many big losses and had to declare bankruptcy. The strain meant that not only did Aidan lose his home but his marriage as well. All he could afford was a one-room bedsit, and in a state of helplessness Aidan turned to alcohol on top of his gambling.

During one of our sessions, Aidan told me of his love for horses as he had grown up with them in his hometown in Southern Ireland. Together, we worked hard to reframe this love away from betting on horses and towards training horses. Aidan simply had the wrong take on his passion, actually being more interested in the statistics and performance of different racing breeds than the gambling itself.

Aidan returned to his hometown in Ireland and over the course of ten years, he built a successful stable of racing horses with his brother. This same man, who had taken such a fall from his previous successful career and lifestyle, had worked his way up on another's stud farm as a trainer to eventually run his own successful business breeding and selling racing horses worth hundreds and thousands of pounds. Now in his sixties, Aidan has re-married and has two children whom he proudly adores. It is never too late to take on new opportunities.

Your favourite excuses

What excuses do you make about your dreams?

- I'm not smart enough?
- It's too difficult?
- I don't have the energy.

- I don't have the time.
- It's too much of a risk?
- I'm too young/too old?
- I'm not well enough/fit enough?
- Life is hard?
- People can't be happy/I can't be happy?
- I'm just unlucky?

Would your list become a page of excuses?

Take anything you want to achieve, and you will find dozens of excuses as to why you should not do it. However, when you want something badly enough, you will do whatever you can to get it! Especially if you know that nothing worthwhile comes without some kind of struggle. A struggle after all is simply a challenge, and challenges are good for us to grow in our personal learning and experience.

What doesn't kill you, makes you stronger! When you are about to give up, say to yourself,

- "Just one more ....!"

See if you can squeeze out just a bit more from your personal discipline.

Exercise 3: Focusing on your strengths

1. Know your answers to the following questions:

- What are my capabilities?
- *(My talents, skills and knowledge)*
- What can't I do that I feel I must or should be able to do?
- *(My perceived weaknesses or current lack of knowledge that I require in my life)*

2. Now ask these more important questions:

- Who told me I can or can't? Myself or someone else?
- What are the real facts behind whether I can or can't?

3. Finally ask:

- Which capability will I focus on making even stronger?
- How exactly will I make this capability even stronger?
- Which weakness will I focus on improving?
- How exactly will I improve this weakness?

Do or Do Not. There is no Try. - Master Yoda

It's time to destroy the weak words and excuses in your life and step up and take responsibility.

NO LONGER ARE you to say the word 'Try'

IT IS a zero word that means nothing! If someone says they will "Try", it is likely they will NOT Try.

- I'll try my best
- I'll try to behave
- I'll try to stop smoking

Replace 'Try' with 'Will'

- I will do my best
- I will behave
- I will stop smoking

Even better, add 'Now'

- I will do my best now

- I will behave now
- I will stop smoking now

You will not succeed by using the word "Try". It is a soft excuse that leads to a potent irresponsible decision to do nothing

"WILL," on the other hand, is a strong word that requires a positive promise to action, motivating your commitment to effort and persistence.

SELF-FULFILLING PROPHECIES AND YOUR UNCONSCIOUS MIND

WHAT YOU DO, FEEL AND SEE IS HOW THINGS WILL BE

H aving earlier introduced the concept of the conscious and unconscious mind, in this chapter we will explore how to utilise your unconscious to make lasting positive changes to increase your levels of happiness.

Change your thinking first

When you change, things around you change as well. That is how your mind works, like attracts like and what you think about will grow. You plant a seed in your mind and the flower that results reflects your thinking. Plant bright sunflowers and that is what you will grow. Sow negative thoughts and weeds will grow, occupying and choking the clarity of your thinking.

What you believe in and pursue will determine your quality of life. Your current situation is a reflection of all you believe now and all you have believed in the past.

If you make a prediction about your future and sincerely believe it, it is likely to come true as you will unconsciously shape that future through your actions or your inaction. This is known as a "Self-Fulfilling Prophecy." Something that doesn't yet exist comes into being as your behaviours align with the thoughts you carry in your mind. This prediction could be negative or positive, depending on your outlook at the time.

This is how an unhappy brain works...

This is what I think the world should be:

- It should be fair!
- It should be quiet!
- It shouldn't be so horrible!

This is how I think people should behave:

- They should be honest!
- They should not be late!
- They should return my favours!
- They should know when I'm unhappy!
- They should be considerate!
- They should remember the last time they did that, and I was not impressed!
- They should know what I am thinking!
- I will be upset and angry if I am not appreciated for my beliefs!

... and this is how a happy brain works

- I would prefer if .... happened, but I will expect that the outcome may be different and I will concentrate on what is in my control and change my approach if I need to.

Exercise 4: Know your limited rules for life

1. List how you believe the world should or shouldn't be or must and mustn't be.
2. Catch your "must" and "should" thoughts and replace them with a more empowering response such as:

I would prefer if ____ happened, but if it doesn't, I will accept it or improve it by changing what is in my control.

Acting is Reacting

When I studied acting in University as part of my first degree, my teacher, Frank Ford, often said that "acting is reacting," a commonly known expression in theatre and film studies.

By reacting to what another is saying, you are actively listening; that is, you are understanding and responding naturally to the message being communicated.

To be an optimistic and positive person, reacting is key to your happiness. You invest a good proportion of your time listening, observing and reacting positively to people and events.

You can't change the world; however, you can easily change your reaction to world events.

The patterns of behaviour and the beliefs we hold in our mind determine whether we make friends easily, make money easily, spot opportunities, readily take risks, get ill all the time, are always broke, and eat unhealthily etc.

By holding certain beliefs such as "People with money have got it by cheating or stealing from others" you are feeding a self-fulfilling prophecy that plays out in your unconscious mind. This means you are unlikely to have more than a comfortable amount of money as you will unconsciously be rid of it by spending it at every opportunity. Your resulting actions are a reaction to your beliefs.

Cause and effect

Our unconscious beliefs are formed from how we have interpreted our past experiences and now motivate the feelings we have and the actions we take in response to current events. Many beliefs have been formed in our past when we were vulnerable children and teenagers. Some are now hidden from our recall to protect us from possible psychological and physical harm.

Phobias are often linked to real or perceived traumas. Acting and reacting is connected to cause and effect. Cause and effect is when one event causes another to happen. The cause is the event and the effect is your response to it. In the case of a phobia, the presence of a spider may cause someone to react with fear and anxiety. This may be due to an actual trauma related to a spider or seeing someone else reacting fearfully to seeing a spider, or a fear developed from a story, image, tv or film.

If your happiness and wellbeing is affected deeply by something from your past, you should always seek professional psychological or medical support for traumas and phobias. If they are buried within your unconscious, a psychology professional should be able to help you explore the source of your fears and then manage them.

A picture of the unconscious mind

The classic image to make sense of our unconscious mind is to imagine an iceberg in the sea. The small tip of the iceberg that protrudes from the water is your conscious mind and represents when you carry out daily activities with full awareness. The bulk of the iceberg lying beneath the surface of the ocean is the unseen unconscious mind which carries out the infinitesimal tasks that your body must coordinate and activate to keep you alive and functioning. This also includes many past memories, all your values, beliefs, thoughts and feelings.

You can also imagine the unconscious this way; if you drive a car, do you think about how you use the brake, clutch and gears? If you ride a bicycle, do you consciously think about balancing and adjusting the steering while you pedal and hurtle down the road? When you breathe do you focus on all the elements that expand and compress your diaphragm, and then circulate the oxygen through your lungs, heart and blood stream?

These are all unconscious processes which are nature-designed for our survival. There are also many practices we have learnt by consciously rehearsing them over-and-over and are now controlled mainly by our automatic unconscious mind. If we had to think about every little thing that we learnt or did all the time, it would take us an eternity just to walk a few steps. If you know your times tables by rote, this is now an unconscious learning, just like any other learning, thought or belief that we now store in our mind.

In the war between your conscious attempts to stop a behaviour and your unconscious belief to continue that behaviour, your unconscious belief will win most of the battles until you have rehearsed the new behaviour over-and-over again. This is because the old behaviour still brings you some level of perceived comfort, even if it is not good for you.

That is why giving up an addiction such as smoking is so difficult. You have to consciously stop smoking that next cigarette until your unconscious accepts the behaviour of not smoking as the new normal. This also applies to negative thinking. If you are in the habit of thinking negatively, you will need to consciously persist with thinking positively at every opportunity to train your unconscious mind to take on positive thinking as your new approach to life.

What you are doing is retraining the network of neurological pathways produced to replicate your present behaviour. By creating a new behaviour through persistent practice, you build a different network within the brain that reinforces this new behaviour. The pathways of the old behaviour gradually reduce in their activity and no longer become a motivator for that old behaviour. Whenever you wish to stop an old behaviour, it is best to replace it and build a new positive behaviour to override the old.

Changing thoughts

The great news is that you can change your thoughts and beliefs. By questioning your old and negative beliefs until you doubt their validity and being aware of the triggers that set your response in motion, you take away the automatic unconscious response to trigger events. By consciously rehearsing better and empowering beliefs in your imagination and in the real world, the new and better beliefs will become automatic and unconscious.

Often, when we are in a state of dreaming, we consider the dream to be a real experience at the time. Studies in the cognitive functions of our mind suggest that our unconscious cannot necessarily distinguish between what is real and what is imaginary. If you are dreading speaking in front of your next work meeting and you have been playing out a scenario in your mind about all that could go wrong and leave you embarrassed, you create a very real nervousness and fear for the event. I have seen people anticipate so much worry before a presentation that they are physically vomiting before they go on. Imagine if they had been generating excitement and pride in their efforts up to their presentation. They would have been eager to hit that stage and give 100% of their hard work.

There are countless things you have consciously learned to do, and once you have become familiar with the practice, your unconscious has taken over activities such as:

- brushing your teeth
- getting dressed
- making a mug of coffee
- emptying the dish washer
- touch-typing
- knitting

Just like athletes who rehearse a perfect high jump or shot-put in their imagination, or an actor going through their lines and rehearsing a scene in their imagination, or learning a speech, or teaching a lesson, we can rehearse new beliefs and situations in our imaginations until they become second-nature.

Exercise 5: Imagining if...

1. Close your eyes and relax for a moment with a few calm breaths.
2. Imagine seeing yourself from a distance walking down the street, smiling and saying 'hello' to your neighbours or to colleagues in your workplace. In this vision, notice how they react positively.
3. Now imagine doing the very same thing as if you are looking through your own eyes. Hear the confident voice coming from you as you say "Hi." Feel the smile from your lips and move it into your eyes. Feel the good feelings that come from positively greeting others. Hear a positive reply coming from each person you greet.

You may have just made somebody's day.
Keep the exercise simple and easy to practice. Try the following:

1. In your imagination, practice being relaxed and calm when speaking with someone who usually causes you to be nervous.
2. Start by seeing yourself at a distance going through a successful scenario.
3. When you are ready, re-run the scene looking through your own eyes and imagine your feelings of confidence and calm.
4. Rehearse whenever you can get a moment.

How to use your imagination for visualisation

You don't need perfect conditions and someone to help you to do it. You can do it on the train or on waking up in the morning. Whatever works for you.

A misconception about mental rehearsal is that to be successful at visualising you need to be able to see things perfectly clear or things have to move like a movie, rather than be still as in a photograph. This is not the case. What you really need for a successful visualisation is to access and feel the feelings you desire now, in the moment, while imagining the future situation. Feel your end goal now, whether it be ease, calm or confidence, your mind is able to powerfully fill in the situations details for you. Remember that the unconscious does not necessarily distinguish what is imagined from what is real. Some have described the unconscious mind as quite literal in its acceptance of events.

Like an athlete of performer, be persistent and practice frequently until things just seem to happen automatically; in other words, your unconscious mind has taken over the conscious task of practicing for you.

The power of words on the unconscious mind

Mind what you say to yourself and others as this also reinforces the images and beliefs in your unconscious mind. I reiterate that the unconscious has been described as literal in what it accepts into your deepest thoughts. These thoughts will be re-enacted in your imagination and will likely play out in your world outside. If you say something negative to yourself, learn to fight back with positive logic:

- "My teacher said I am not very bright."
- *Did they really say that or is it my interpretation? If they did, that was inappropriate behaviour for a teacher and they have a problem. We all learn through practice which takes effort and perseverance.*

- "I never have enough ...."
- *There is plenty for everyone, you just need to learn the same or similar actions to what others are doing to get the same or similar results.*
- "I'm hopeless ...."
- *Really? Who says? Where is the evidence? Are you only "hopeless" and nothing else? What are some things you are good at?*
- "I can't lose the fat from my body, no matter what I do."
- *I'm sure you can, we all can unless there is the tiny chance we have a medical condition that needs professional treatment. What sensible things have other people followed to really lose body fat? Am I truly maintaining a consistent healthy diet and exercising, or am I inconsistent?*

Only say good things about yourself and when you hear others running themselves down, tell them "Of course you can!" and "Of course you have!" and "Of course you are!" and follow up with an "I believe in you and what you are capable of doing!" If you can say this to others, you can also say this to yourself.

What is your intention for running yourself down with negative comments?

Self-criticism is typically vocalised to others as a signal for help, a signal for attention and a signal for connection. You can help yourself and others by questioning the source of the belief, figuring out if there is any REAL evidence behind that belief, and offering a positive self-fulfilling prophecy in its place.

USE the following acronym to keep things REAL:
Requires
Evidence
Affirming

Likelihood

WHICH MEANS the probability that something is real is very high.

QUESTION Every negative thought and don't allow them to run roughshod over your right to feel good about yourself.

"I just can't be happy"

- Who says?
- What's the source of your thinking?
- What has happened to make you feel this way?
- Have you never been happy before?
- What does happiness meant to you?
- What exactly do you need to experience in order to feel happy?
- If I could wave a magic wand and make you happy, what will have changed in how you think and see your life?

Like attracts like

Have you ever bumped into someone when you were just thinking about them in the most unlikely place? Have you ever just been thinking of someone and they phone you out of the blue?

- If you focus on the colour blue, you will see it everywhere.
- If you suddenly fancy a certain item you want to buy, suddenly you'll find it all around you, compelling you to buy it.

What you focus on becomes a self-fulfilling prophecy on a like attracts like basis. Happy people attract happy people and miserable people attract miserable people.

Your thoughts and dreams are very real, they can transform your reality. If you support a certain political party, all you will notice are other supporters reinforcing what you believe in. Recently, this has become very real with the advent of digitally targeted media online. Like your mind, computer algorithms know your online search habits and your basic identity profile. Your casual internet browsing serves up exactly what you want to see or believe in the form of product advertising and news. In fact, you are now treated as a product too! Your digital profile being sold by data collection services to companies who want to place their adverts in front of you in the hope of making a sale!

The amazing aspect of digital media being served straight to our digital devices is the fact that they travel vast distances and appear right before our eyes in an instant. This information are like thoughts broken into digital 0's and 1's travelling through time and space. Our thoughts are the same. They are produced by the chemicals in our mind yet have a profound influence over the directions we take in life. It is all so magical and much still unexplainable at the writing of this book, yet we understand enough about the mind to make it work to our positive advantage. We must always consider, then choose, the positive and the good and then we will experience more happiness in our lives.

If you see yourself having good and true friends, they will enter your life. See yourself achieving something you desire, and if you truly want it, you will work toward it and bring it to life.

Anti-action words

When visualising, be wary of the words DON'T and DO NOT

Our unconscious mind has difficulty understanding negatives, that is words that negate actions.

When I was around the age of 10, I was at a friend's house and he was showing me their new stove top which to me was just a smooth piece of magical black glass. He turned it on, and the red elements began to glow. He then said, "Whatever you do don't touch it!" For some reason beyond my conscious common sense, I touched it, and the next thing I had my hand under a running cold water tap to ease the blistering that was already appearing on my fingertips. Why?

In my head I unconsciously did not hear "don't", it was like my mind heard "Whatever you do, touch it!"

This is a pretty consistent phenomena in scientific studies of unconscious thinking and it is highly utilised in hypnosis, neuro-linguistic programming and cognitive-behavioural therapy to create change in people.

"DON'T RELAX TOO QUICKLY!"

"DO not give up biting your nails as you know it isn't good for you, DON'T you!"

IT IS common in our own day-to-day lives as well.

DON'T tell me what to do!

DON'T do that!

That is NOT the way to do it!

DO not enter!

THESE ARE the kind of words that cause a mental rebellion because they stir our curiosity. Who could resist the temptation of the following?

"I'VE PLACED a bowl of chocolates on the table for when our guests arrive. I'm just going out for a minute, whatever you DO, DO not eat them!"

Don't be the martyr, just ask for support

One fear that a number of people hold is appearing needy to others and relying on their help. They feel that they are using that person and taking away their time. However, happy and successful people seem able to ask for help without hesitation. It is because they see the good in people and feel that they are not an imposition. Happy people also do not feel they are being imposed upon when others ask for help; instead, they are delighted to give assistance.

This is the mindset of a person who gets on and accomplishes their goals. There is no issue in asking for help, and more-often-than-not, you will receive that help or at least a point in the right direction. Just ensure that you are willing to help others when they ask. If someone does say "No," it is not personal, and you simply move on to ask someone else.

- "Can you warm my coffee up; it's a little cold and I prefer it hot?"
- "Since I have been buying my car insurance with you for a while, can you offer me a discount?"
- "Could you offer me a sample/trial of this as I will possibly buy it if it works out right for me?"
- "I was wondering if I could approach you for some advice as I know you are an expert on the subject?"

YOU DON'T GET if you don't ask and you have the right to ask as long as you keep in mind not to expect that everyone will help you.

Some people who work hard do so for years without asking for a pay rise, whereas others who don't work nearly as much or for as long, ask for a pay rise and receive it. It is often not personal, it is just that someone asked for that raise before you did. We cannot expect life to be automatically fair without our own efforts involved. Be brave and frame everything you ask in a positive light along the lines of the benefits you offer, "I have recently been praised for my work here and I am very loyal to the company, can we look at a figure for a raise in my salary?"

Scarcity and abundance

Often, we imagine what we won't have in the future rather than what we will have in abundance. This is known as "scarcity thinking." You predict the worst result for yourself before anything even happens. You think there is not enough on offer out there in the world for you to get a fair share of. As we know, our thoughts have an influence over our reality. Our thoughts create our circumstances.

The opposite of "scarcity thinking" is "abundance thinking." Abundance is believing that there is enough in our world for everyone. It is another belief that Happy people live their lives by. They never feel that they will miss out, because there is an abundance of what they seek in the world. What happy people seek are more positive feelings and sharing it with other people. Many people doubt the abundance theory and that makes some sense as they view abundance not as energy but as limited material resources.

Happy people may see abundance in the number of:

- other positive and giving people in the world
- fun experiences to be enjoyed
- people doing good things to help the planet
- people living in peace

A PERSON SEEING scarcity will see the opposite in the number of:

- negative news reports about the world
- negative and selfish people in the world
- people doing bad things to others and the environment

- people living in war and unrest

Sure, there are a lot of negative events occurring in the world at any one time, but there is always a positive path we can follow to improve things for future events involving the environment or other people. You will find that more positive and happy people take action in influencing or inspiring change than negative people who state their worries and concerns but take no action. The positive people see the opportunities for change and the negative people see that nothing can be done and blame and complain.

Not everything can be seen or understood

Just because we can't see things, does not mean they do not exist; the concept of scarcity and abundance plays a big part in our world.

Our current scientific understanding and theories of the Universe helps us to put how little we still know into perspective.

Scientists propose that there may be other unseen dimensions connected to our world but there may be several different reasons that we don't see them. Here are just a few:

- They are possibly so tiny they are beyond our sight and microscopic equipment.
- They are inaccessible to all our senses.
- The fabric of their existence is so warped that they can't be discerned.

How come there is such a far-fetched concept of different dimensions in our Universe? String theorists have an understanding of the Universe that some certain concepts are in existence but can only work properly in nine or more dimensions of space and one dimension of time.

There are many unsolved areas of physics that are proven in theory and should be physically present and test-able in our dimension, but are absent. The reason for their absence may be because they play across other dimensions, and therefore we cannot fathom them in our world, such as dark matter and black holes.

To further illustrate the unknown and unseen forces of our Universe, physics suggests that the future has already happened through the concept of "The Block Universe." All the things that have happened, are happening and will happen already exist and our passage through time is just a function of our perception.

The concept of distance can also warp our understanding of how we understand time. The Andromeda Galaxy is 2,000,000 light years away, so what we see of the Andromeda Galaxy now is also 2,000,000 years old. This means that we are having visions of the past and not what is currently in existence in the galaxy's now.

A closer to home phenomenon, sound and light travels to us at different speeds, yet we often perceive them as synced together. Distant lightning strikes first before we hear the thunder from the breaking of the sound barrier. when the lightning strikes directly near us, we hear the thunderclap at the same time as the lightning strike.

The smallest particle is still not a certainty. We know in descending size order that there are atoms, a nucleus, electrons, protons, neutrons, and recently quarks; but what is smaller than a quark is currently unknown as we don't yet have the ability to measure anything smaller.

Darkness also seems to be a limitation to what we can see around us. If we could see in infrared, we would never experience complete darkness again, even in what we would consider pitch black. Everything in the Universe is glowing at one temperature or another and every temperature has an infrared colour. White is perceived at 1300 degrees Celsius, Orange at 950 degrees Celsius, Red at 650 degrees Celsius which we can see. If we could see in infrared, blues and purples would also be present to our eye, there would be no darkness.

Since the Universe is mainly 95% dark energy and scientists do not yet comprehend the makeup of dark matter, this means that only

5% of the Universe is understood. So for all that is known, there is still much to understand.

WE CAN HOWEVER COME to the conclusion that the source of our existence is energy and we are mainly beings of energy. We are physically made up from the particles of the Universe since its inception. Those same particles will return to the Universe when our physical body is dead.

The Universe is energy and the force of life is energy too. Just as our thoughts are chemical constructs of energy in our mind, our thoughts activate an energy that precedes our feelings and motivates our behaviour.

Good things will happen to you when you feel good and bad things will happen to you when you feel bad, so which energy do you want passing through you? It is your choice after all, and it is one of the only choices in your life under your direct control.

The energy of childhood

Imagine being a child again. Children don't block the flow of the energy of their thoughts, instead they readily enact their imaginative ideas in the physical world. Children don't say, "This is too difficult," they just get along and have a go. Children can learn things so quickly without the critical screening filters we have as adults. In a dual-language home, children naturally pick up both languages.

If a child is raised in a neglectful home where they are exposed to limited language, learning and love, their intellectual, social and emotional growth will be reduced, their energy has been disrupted and their creativity stifled. What you say will slip into a child's unconscious without resistance. If you tell a child that they are clever at maths or a wonderful reader, this is what will go into their unconscious. If you say that they need to do better, they are to blame for something, or they annoy you, this will also go into their unconscious beliefs. Childhood is the source of many of our issues; the criticisms, intended or not, that you heard and accepted as a child from your family, friends, school mates, teachers and other authority figures. These laws remain embedded in your psyche and dictate the way you react to the world, until they are consciously challenged.

The unconscious is like a child

The unconscious mind does not think or challenge or debate what it hears, the information slips into your mind to be used as instructions, often quite literally.

When you plant a thought, your unconscious grows from this thought, creating patterns of behaviour that seem to be compulsive, reactive and out of your control. These unconscious patterns are why history often repeats itself. This is the reason why:

- People become even more successful each day that passes, whilst others seem to never touch success.
- People seem to always have money that grows every day, while others appear to spiral further downward into debt.
- People seem to date many partners while other people can't even seem to find one relationship.
- People live in happiness and others in misery.

THE GREAT NEWS is that you do not have to follow past patterns. You do not need to ruminate on past events and feel guilt, shame or regret over them. Whatever burdens you now, you have picked up in life. You can now decide to unload them and carry them no longer. Start responding to present events with new positivity, happiness and a smile deep inside with the knowledge that you have the chance to begin again.

. . .

YOUR INTERNAL THOUGHTS create positive or negative energy and like attracts like. Your thoughts will become real for you, whether in your view of the world or in your physical reality. Something comes from seemingly nothing. Thoughts seed into beliefs which become actions. The creation of our Universe is the most powerful example of the seemingly nothing becoming an incredible physical construct. Professor Stephen Hawking said:

"THE ENTIRE, enormous Universe, all the innumerable galaxies, even time and space and the forces of nature themselves, simply materialised out of nothing."

IF WE BRING this into a human context:

- What will stress, anger, frustration, worry, doubt, paranoia, and anxiety materialise into?
- What will joy, positivity, love, passion, calm, peace and happiness materialise into?

If you are always asking "Something will go wrong?" something will go wrong!

If you are always saying "Things will get better." Things will eventually get better.

THE BUDDHA SAID,
"With our thoughts, we make the world."

Decide what you want and feel the feelings of already achieving it

To get what you want, you have to know what you want, believe in what you want and act on what you want with the knowledge that each action will bring you closer to it. You must aim your positive energy in the direction you want to go through the actions you take, not hold it inside of you just wishing and hoping for things to get better.

In your imagination you visualise your want as if you already have it and experience the feeling of having achieved it, right now. These positive and happy feelings become powerful motivators for you to confidently start taking action. If you are one who prays, pray as if the prayer is already answered and give thanks for receiving it.

These are the happy self-fulfilling prophecies you must create. How you feel is the key to the positive energy that you put out into the world and the energy that you receive back from the world. Words are useless without the positive and happy feelings behind them which spur you on to action.

It is very difficult to fix the problems in your life when you feel bad about them. Your first step is to feel good, to feel hope and then go about making the repairs required.

Affirmations

Affirmations can bring change when you enhance them with specific strong feelings, acknowledge that you can already have it, and state how things will be even better:

- "I am rich!" is pretty vague compared to "I already have most of what I need in life and I excitedly feel my investments expanding and improving every day."
- "I am happy!" is expanded to "I'm feeling happier every day because I appreciate things more and I now positively manage any challenges."
- "I am confident!" is expanded to "I feel growing daily confidence as I respond to any resistance from my calm centre of control."

Exercise 6: Creating personally specific positive affirmations

With a manageable list of 3 or less, list the responses you wish to improve using better feelings:

Create an affirmation for each by answering the following questions:

1. What positive feeling do you wish to experience?
2. When do you wish to experience it?
3. Why will things be better with this empowering feeling?
4. Turn your affirmation into a memorable "I feel" sentence.

FOR EXAMPLE:

1. I want to feel happy.
2. When communicating with others.
3. It will put people at ease and build rapport.
4. I feel happier each day knowing that when I speak with others with a smile on my face they feel more open and at ease in my presence.

Lightening and brightening when you feel only darkness

If you still genuinely struggle with feeling any light or happiness in your life, practicing the following imaginative exercise can be very effective if you do it daily.

Exercise 7: Warm golden light

A tiny bit of hope can take you a long way. It is like the power of that little ray of sunlight piercing through a stormy sky. This little seed of a positive feeling can be nurtured and grown. We can bring a feeling of sunshine into our lives even on the gloomiest of days.

In this simple exercise, begin by finding a space where you can close your eyes.

1. Imagine feeling a gentle, warm ray of sunlight on the top of your head.
2. Now imagine the golden sunlight filling and warming your body starting from the top of your head and moving all throughout your body, down to your toes.
3. Notice the warm glow as it radiates throughout your body and how this makes you feel. Feeling the feeling is more important than getting the visualisation clear or 'right' in your mind. A strong, positive and happy feeling holds the most power for change.
4. If you find the feeling of warmth difficult to experience, you can try imagining a pure, gentle and energising beam of white light appearing as a ray from the sky above. It moves into your head gently energising your body as it travels through you until you are completely aglow with pure white light.

Your contribution for a better world

Feelings reveal our inner thoughts and state of mind. What we project out to the world is what we will attract more of. Whatever you have in your life right now, you created yourself. Whatever you wish to create or change, you will create for yourself. When you change how you feel, you change what you receive more of on a like for like basis.

A KEY to creating a better world for yourself and others is what you are capable of contributing right now using the HAPPY acronym:

- Happiness through a smile and acceptance of others.

- Appreciation through genuine compliments and thankfulness.
- Positivity by looking at the bright side of a challenging event.
- Pardon for your own mistakes and those of others.
- Yourself: you full attention and what you can offer.

How to quickly create happy feelings physically

Physiologically, one of the quickest and easiest ways to get yourself into a positive state of mind is to stand up straight and tall, take a deep breath in and out to calm yourself and smile. Remember, "Dress your best when you feel your worst." In many situations a smile will solve many problems including your own. Even a forced smile will engage feelings of happiness. A smile does not need to be open-mouthed and stretched wide, you may have your lips together. You can even practice bringing a smile into your eyes. It has the same effect as a full smile on lifting your mood and evoking happy feelings.

Even better, a wink and a smile.

In my early years of employment, I worked for a while in a job centre with people who were unemployed and seeking work.

Understandably, being unemployed can bring feelings of frustration, upset and anger as seeking work carries many challenges related to money, accommodation, relationships, self-worth and general wellbeing. I learned from one of my managers how to best help jobseekers experiencing difficult feelings even when there was little to offer. She would stand tall, smile, greet the client cheerfully, and listen. Not in a condescending way but in an understanding way. She genuinely felt for all who came to her desk and she would always do as much as she could to help and explain what she was unable to help with. Even the angriest person could see her sincerity and would eventually calm down. Whenever I saw another colleague being defensive with an unemployed client, communication would quickly break down, voices would be raised and even threats exchanged. Your chances of harmony with others is highest from a happy and understanding state than from a defensive or confrontational position. This is not manipulation if you genuinely understand people and mean how you feel.

When you have to make a phone call that you've been dreading, keep a smile on your face as you are speaking, even when the situation calls for a serious conversation, a smile will keep you positive and looking for solutions rather than more problems. It is very difficult to be pulled into the negatives of a conversation when you have a smile on your face.

When you have to enter a room to face a new situation or a difficult situation, take a deep breath, hold it and then breathe out before you enter. As you enter, stand tall and keep a small smile on your face. This has the quick effect of centring you and opening you up to being stronger and more positive to what may eventuate. Standing tall physically opens up all your bodily organs and holding your chin up very slightly gives you a quick boost of energy and confidence. If you look downward most of the time, you will notice a positive difference to your feelings when you lift you gaze higher. The word "uplifting" literally means being lifted upright as you are inspired by happy feelings.

If you are about to experience a difficult or awkward situation and you are aware of its possibility, how do you want to face it? In a resigned, weak and powerless way? Or in an upright, positive and open way, with a feeling of happiness that reflects your personal strength and integrity?

The best Self-fulfilling prophecies are born from positive choice and taking action

There is a positive choice out there in the world and a negative choice as well. Positive and happy people focus on the positive choices only, whilst unhappy and negative people pick up on all the negative choices and then complain about them. You are also the source of giving out positive or negative choices to others, through your actions and the things you say.

- What benefits do you get from giving out negative replies, commands or questions?
- Why is this a benefit for leading a happy and positive life?

What you express outward is a projection of your inner state and a reflection of positive and trusting feelings or negative and suspicious feelings.

By giving your best in a positive and happy way, you are giving out good energy to the world. If you hold it inside, your gifts are lost. There are plenty of successful people out there in our world who we see praised in the media, and there are many, many more of us whose undiscovered talents are lost in the masses. It is estimated that the untapped talent that lies out in the world, eclipses the talents of those currently in the public eye. Maybe you have something more to offer the world than you give yourself the credit for?

You change when you believe you can

Just over 15 years ago I was working with a young man who experienced a heart attack at work while in his twenties.

Max had a genetic, undiagnosed condition with one of his heart valves. Having built a career in the IT industry as a Project Manager, he was earning very well. The experience of having a heart attack at work left Max with PTSD (Post Traumatic Stress Disorder), and he was unable to return to the busy and demanding role for fear of having another heart attack, plus the association of having had it in his workplace. Cardiologists assured him that he was young, fit and the surgery had restored the proper function of his valve, however his fears persisted. So much so, that Max moved back with his parents and was slowly going into debt, no longer interested in IT. He was also worried that he would never find love as, "Who would go out with someone who might not live for very long?"

Even I had difficulties working with him as any mention of improving, fixing, feeling better would send him into a state of panic about his heart being "broken." Max's aversion to his work and the stress and hours around him led us to exploring other loves in his life.

As a child, he had accomplished stage 8 in piano and he still had a passion for playing. His love was for jazz, but he felt that because his training was mainly through site-reading classical pieces, he didn't have the free-flowing improvisational technique to play it. We discussed what made his skill at playing piano any different than others who improvised and Max came to the conclusion that he just needed to let go and flow, without following the rules.

Expanding this idea of letting go and not following rules, I was able to reframe Max's view that all of our life happens within just this moment, like the free-flow of jazz, there is no future and no past. We only have the present moment and thinking of the past is pointless and the future is unknown. Max left our last session with a seed of a philosophy that life is like jazz, an improvisation where you can travel confidently from one note to the next by letting go of trying to control what has gone before and what is yet to come.

When Max contacted me a few years later, he told me that at the time of leaving my session, he felt elated as he had written a list of all the things he wanted in life and had rehearsed them in his mind as if he already had them. He wanted a job that wasn't based around stress, and to meet a partner who understood this too. Max retrained as a music teacher and was working in a school which he said was the most rewarding experience of his life. He said that the following belief, which I instil in a number of my clients, stuck with him and was a turning point for his life. It is along the lines of:

"Every day we build on what we already have and let go of the thoughts of things we don't have. Successful people lack many skills, but they take strong action with the skills they do have!"

Max had also been working as a jazz pianist in several groups and it was in one of these groups where he met his partner, a jazz singer. He said that their life was filled with music.

By refocusing his thoughts and seeing life from a moment-to-moment perspective, Max was no longer living in the fear of what might happen in the future, and what a beautiful metaphor that his life is like jazz.

Accepting and choosing life

I, like everyone else, have experienced extremely rough patches in my life, from break-ups to the death of people close to me. I have survived my own personal health scares, including cancer and my own unexpected heart attack. It was having met people like Max, who made my recovery faster with a growing feeling of hope. What gets me through difficulties is an unwavering optimism and genuine happiness and appreciation for the good in life.

Life is not predictable and no matter who you are, rich, poor, healthy, unhealthy, successful or struggling, you are just as prone to external events as the rest of us. This is not said to cause you fear. It is the reality of being alive. When you accept that life is what it is, you can begin to appreciate what you have and choose to be positive and happy in each moment that goes by.

The Stoic Philosophers used to visualise death in order to give them a realistic view of life and appreciating the present moment. The Victorians used to have a fascination with death, including posing in photographs with their dead relatives and some having real human skulls in their houses to remind them to appreciate life now. A number paintings of the time contain a human skull as a reminder of our impermanence. We have lost touch with death as much of it happens out of our view behind a curtain in a hospital. The preparation for the funeral is completed without our involvement. In earlier historical days, death would have been much closer to us all as people died at home or at work. This continues to occur in less-developed, poorer countries, and war zones.

Exercise 8: Creating the motivation to get started

Imagine how powerful your self-fulfilling prophecies would be if you appreciated your life now because you knew that each moment of your life is precious. Imagine how you would lose your fear if you knew that as long as you survive, nothing is a real threat. Death is the real end, worrying about being embarrassed, uncomfortable or making a mistake is trivial in comparison.

1. Imagine if you were given a limited time to live, perhaps 6 months. What would you consider important to achieve within that time before you passed?
2. If you knew you were going to die soon, what would you appreciate more in your day-to-day life?
3. What regrets do you think you might have if your life was about to end?

Keeping your eventual death in mind, let's get to the nitty-gritty of how you should be living:

1. What do you need to start appreciating now?
2. How do you need to live your life now knowing you have the opportunity to change?
3. What do you need to stop doing in your life now?
4. What do you need to start doing in your life now?

Making mountains out of molehills

When we think everything is bad or going wrong, it usually isn't. We just haven't put things into the perspective of,

• "What is the worst thing that could happen?"

Knowing that you will handle most of the worst things is comfort.

Your current work, relationships, and happiness are not the be all and end all of life. They can be changed through starting to choose positive options. Bit-by-bit, the positive choices and actions will build, and your personality will be transformed into a positive and happy thinker more often than not.

.   .   .

LIFE IS like rowing a boat down a flowing stream. We have no control over the flowing currents, just as we have no real control over external events. Much debris floating around us passes by and some occasionally strikes the vessel causing us concern and sometimes damage. However, we still have the ability to steer from side-to-side from one moment in time to the next, using our oars to avoid and deflect many of the obstacles.

One oar represents your feelings and the other oar your beliefs, and they work best together, with strength and consistency. Positive actions help you avoid the debris through positive reactions. If you can't be bothered with the effort and negatively resign yourself to giving up your oars, you will bump into every obstacle that comes along until you end up on the rocks. Positive reactions to difficult events lead you toward calmer waters but it does take effort and persistence.

4

A HAPPIER SELF-ESTEEM

YOU ARE SHAPED BY WHO YOU THINK YOU ARE AND WHAT
YOU THINK YOU ARE NOT

In Psychology, Self-Esteem is defined as your personal overall
feeling of self-worth and value in the world; how much you like
and appreciate yourself. Considered a personality trait, there are 3
common forms:

1. An inflated self-esteem when someone believes they are
   better than others. They can do no wrong and will blame
   others or external forces for their mistakes.
2. A high self-esteem when someone values and accepts
   themselves. They take responsibility and action, and are
   not concerned about what others may think of them. This
   is a balanced and healthy self-esteem.
3. A low self-esteem when someone doesn't value themselves
   and underestimates their capabilities. They rely on others'
   approval and fear failure under other people's eyes.

As a person who chooses happiness, you accept yourself for who
you are without comparing your shortfalls to others' strengths. You fit
into the Goldilocks Zone, not too inflated, not too low, just right. You
know that your reactions to events are within your control and to

think anything negatively is a pointless pre-occupation. No matter what your position in life, you will ensure you'll enjoy it and make use of the strengths that you have; there is no wishing for things that you know are out of your control and simply not guaranteed. You will make the best of what you can actually change and inspire change using the best of your beliefs and skills.

If you fall into the low self-esteem description and act in fear of what other people might think of you, remember that you can change a thought. You cannot live a life making assumptions about what people are thinking of you. By learning to change your negative thoughts to positives, you begin to discover your strengths which makes you much more effective in your daily life. If you begin looking for the silver lining along the edge of a dark cloud, you are going to find ways to overcome obstacles to your happiness.

Put your needs first

For the world to provide you good opportunities, you have to be open to and recognise them first. Then take those opportunities even if you feel for those who might miss out. You are not being selfish, you are putting yourself into a more helpful position where one day you can choose to provide opportunities for someone else. It is very difficult to help others with their needs when you have not met your own first.

Peace of mind doesn't come from having less problems, it comes from being less critical, first with yourself and then with others. When they present the emergency procedures on an airplane, you are instructed to first put your oxygen mask on before helping others. In first aid training you are instructed to ensure your own safety first before aiding another in an accident. Many people have drowned by throwing themselves into dangerous waters to attempt a rescue of a stranger and even a pet. Imagine the impact on your own family losing you in this situation. How can you help others if you are no longer present?

In most situations, putting yourself first isn't being selfish, it is necessary so that you can help from a more effective position.

Exercising your basic rights

We have the basic right to ensure our own best survival as long as it is not at the expense or harm of others who mean us no harm. You cannot guarantee anything outside of you own attitudes and reactions to events. Expect that in a threatening environment or a country that is ruled in a corrupt manner, you rights will be compromised and you have to manage your survival. Know the current International Human Rights Act, which are ideally designed to protect every single person living in our world:

- The right to equality and freedom from discrimination.
- The right to life, liberty, and personal security.
- Freedom from torture and degrading treatment.
- The right to equality before the law.
- The right to a fair trial.
- The right to privacy.
- Freedom of belief and religion.
- Freedom of opinion.

Living your truth and sharing it with like-minded people

Many of us behave differently to please those we encounter in our different day-to-day environments, often at the sacrifice of our core beliefs and values. I am sure you have heard the following many times before,

- "Be true to yourself!" or
- "To thine own self be true."

It is important to show the integrity and congruency of your beliefs and values. This does not mean manipulating, hurting or exploiting others. What you put out into the world should be a reflection of your positive inner self. If you want to put hurt out there, then there is likely an issue that a Psychology professional can help you address.

Your truth should not be affected by your looks and status. You have to operate from your high level of self-esteem. Do not think that celebrities have things easier. They are human too and are exposed to more criticism and trolling than most people. If you have ever questioned your appearance, talents and environment, know that you are in the company of most people. Those who have achieved what you want, also had, and still have their doubts. Often, the persona we see in the media of a person we look up to is nothing like the actual person we imagine. There is much acting required to meet the expectations to remain popular in the media's eyes; "celebrity" is sold like a product.

Beauty in terms of appearance, talent or the actions of an individual, is in the eye of the beholder. What you admire and respect in someone is your opinion; there are others who will take exception to that same person and possibly even dislike them. We cannot expect people to like or admire the same things that we are interested in. Enjoy what you enjoy and share your enjoyment with like-minded people. You will feel much happier communicating with your tribe of like-minded people than expressing your devotion with a critic. Usually, most people are not really interested in your passion for your interests, as they have their own; unless they ask.

Looks are not everything and beauty is in the eye of the beholder. Many actors, comedians and singers are not physically attractive, they are talented actors, comedians and singers. We watch them and listen to them for their talented performance and skill. What they usually have in common with one another is a lot of hard work and a drive to succeed in their profession. They have succeeded by relying on their resilience in the face of rejection or by the vary rare circumstance of chance. Chances are increased by taking or creating many possible opportunities for "Being in the right place at the right time." This is still no guarantee of success and their success still does not mean everyone will like them or that their success will continue. As we all exercise our personal preferences, our human tendency is to serve our own interests above others.

No matter how well prepared we are, how skilled we are, whether we are the best of the best, someone will disagree with the value of our abilities, views or actions.

This rule applies to us all, and the only way to get over it is to realise it and accept it, and not take it personally. It is the secret for building our esteem. We have our preferences and others have theirs. Not everybody has to like us, and we don't have to like everyone else. Learn to respect another's disagreement, there are always similar thoughts we can agree on. Compromise is born from acknowledging many points of view. Always react in a civil way, replying from a positive perspective, even if we don't like the behaviour or beliefs of the person before us.

Very difficult people

What is the solution for dealing with people who take exception to you in any way, shape or form?

Expect that you will come across people who take exception to you. They may have a very low-frustration tolerance to people who are different from them, therefore you cannot take it personally. It is not your problem to solve, it is their personal problem. If you are work colleagues, then the difficult relationship should be mediated by management or the Human Resources Department if you have one. If not, if you are part of a workplace union, they can provide support. If their behaviour is threatening, you need to seek police or legal support. At every opportunity focus on being around the people who share your opinions and enjoy your company.

When meeting with a difficult person who you feel you can manage personally, knowing their preferences of beliefs or behaviours can help you identify the positive similarities between you. This does not mean you abandon your own opinions, it means that you focus on the similarities. When you can relate to your similarities, you can facilitate rapport and communicate in a more harmonious way.

Rapport comes from:

- Having a mutual interest in speaking with one another, i.e. you both are gaining from the conversation.
- You both share a positive approach which is friendly, caring and shows concern for one another. There is no blocking the conversation from either party.
- You are in synchronicity or 'sync' with one another as you naturally and unconsciously match your body language, tone of voice, pace and energy. To an observer, they would notice that you both appear to be mirroring one another.
- You both feel trust.

How do you establish rapport when in conversation?

- Smile.
- Use open body language, not folded arms and legs.
- Mirror in a not too obvious way how the other person is standing and gesturing. Mirror the pace of their voice.
- Ask for and then occasionally use the other person's name as it shows you remember them.
- Listen first and then speak in a give-and-take conversation. Do not dominate the conversation.
- Find similarities, the common ground upon which you can both feel comfortable.
- Be empathetic and concerned. Listen, but don't give advice unless asked.

How to find common ground:

Take notice of your common surroundings and use them as an opener:

- "It's quite warm in here, how do you find it?"

- "Did you have as much difficulty as I did finding this place?"
- "There's quite a crowd today isn't there?"

Notice what they are wearing, how they style their hair, their accessories and comment or ask a question in a sincere, not an overly-personal, creepy or condescending way.

- "I was thinking of getting the same phone. What's the camera on it like?"
- "I like your colourful tie/shirt/dress. It brightens up the room. I have a shirt at home in similar colours which always gets everyone's attention."

When you are asked a question, answer it and add a tag question to keep the conversation flowing:

- Them: "Have you travelled far to be here?"
- You: "Yes I came by train from London. It took me about an hour to get here. *What was your journey like?*"

As the conversation flows ask specific questions that you can both relate to, starting with yourself first and then seek their response:

- "I really enjoy these work conventions, what's your favourite thing about them?"
- "I've always wanted to write a book. What do you find is the best part about being a writer?"
- "I get a little anxious in crowds, yet you seem so calm. How do you remain so relaxed?"

How to deal with criticism constructively

When I was in my teens and early twenties, I worked as an actor in many theatre performances and quickly realised that when you are on public display, you are subject to criticism and critical reviews. Even when a show was panned by critics, there was always at least one review from someone who liked it. Even when dozens of reviews were full of praise, there was also one review that would be largely negative.

In theatre and performance, there is a well-known saying that,

"You can't please all your audience!"

You must focus on the positive to improve the negative when the feedback you receive is constructive.

Both positive and negative criticism is feedback and feedback is to be used constructively. If feedback is malicious and given by people who gain pleasure from putting you down, you must not give them that satisfaction of worrying about it or giving it any of your time. It has no value.

How do we discern the quality of feedback and what should we do?

Think of the positive seed of a habit, skill or talent that you that you are trying to grow. Just as plants take time to grow, so does learning a new subject and practice. Feedback in the form of criticism can be viewed like rain watering a seed. A gentle rain will help that seed to germinate and grow, just as we choose to accept gentle feedback, examine it, learn from it and then take action to improve our growth. Gentle feedback comes from a good critic whose preference for your performance or behaviour to improve is to everyone's benefit. You see, a critic has their own ideal viewpoint of what constitutes a good performance and the right behaviour. They want you to meet their ideal viewpoint if you desire their praise.

Now think of the effect of harsh rain. Harsh rain will wash away the protective and nourishing soil and that seed will not be able to grow. Harsh criticism usually comes in the form of the critic undermining or lambasting you personally. When personalised feedback is harsh, we need to recognise the intent to damage our growth and know that the problem lies in the giver and not us, they are gaining some kind of upper-hand over us through their put-downs. It is simply abusive. A personal attack will leave you with no way of improving your performance if you take it on board. The best you can do is recognise it for what it is and realise that this person is at fault, and you are not. The criticiser has underlying problems relating to, and communicating with, other people. It goes against our basic human rights and we must not and will not store it in our minds, nor dwell upon it. Instead, we can choose to be proactive and report it to an authority or see it for what it is and let that negative energy go.

9 times out of 10, I have had clients whose self-esteem has been affected deeply by discipline taken in a school or workplace. In employment law, an employer is allowed to address the way we behave in their workplace if we are clearly aware of it through a contract or duty statement and our behaviour affects their business. This is presented to us as feedback about our conduct. An employer can also address our capability, that is whether we meet the performance requirements of our job as per our contract. They are not allowed to criticise us personally, only our behaviours and actions can be addressed. However, they must give us a clear warning first before taking any further action. References made about our race, culture, age, disability, gender, sexual orientation, religion or belief, marital situation, and pregnancy, is viewed as discrimination, and in many countries it is illegal.

Identity, character and integrity

To be happy, we must protect the integrity of our character. Our character is the sum of our beliefs and our values which shapes our habits and our morality. We present as a whole being: body, mind and consciousness, and to betray ourselves by compromising the things we uphold is breaching our personal integrity. This is when your self-esteem can drop rapidly. We all have our identity and to lose a sense of it creates anxiety. We can appear to others as unhappy, incongruent, untrustworthy, unstable. or all over the place By betraying our identity we can feel negative emotions such as shame, guilt and regret. If you sense a loss of identity, revisit and reclaim your values and beliefs and importantly forgive yourself for having lost touch with yourself. Give yourself the chance to improve again by exploring your deepest thoughts. While examining those thoughts, choose to do so from a positive perspective and be happy that you now have a chance to renew.

Exercise 9: Discover your Character

You aren't born with a definite identity and character; much of it is made, and it guides your very self-esteem. If you want to truly respect yourself, and earn the respect of others, appearance, education and talent should not be the defining factor. Develop your character and focus on those inner strengths that you uphold, such as courage, determination, honesty, and persistence. These may only seem like words on the surface, however these words have strong feelings, beliefs and thoughts behind them, which we want to be our source of personal power.

See if you recognise any of the following traits that you already live by, or want to live by. Add any others.

BELIEFS, Morals and Values Character Traits

- Accepting
- Brave
- Compassion
- Considerate
- Courageous
- Gentle

- Giving
- Hard-worker
- Honest
- Humble
- Independent
- Leader
- Loyal
- Persistent
- Responsible
- Self-confident
- Selfless

EMOTIONAL AND PHYSICAL Character Traits

- Able
- Busy
- Conceited
- Dainty
- Dark
- Expert
- Fighter
- Gentle
- Handsome
- Imaginative
- Joyful
- Light
- Messy
- Mischievous
- Neat
- Patriotic
- Plain
- Poor
- Popular

- Pretty
- Prim
- Proper
- Rich
- Short
- Strong
- Successful
- Tall
- Tireless
- Ugly
- Wild

PERSONALITY CHARACTER TRAITS

- Adventurous
- Ambitious
- Bossy
- Bright
- Cheerful
- Cooperative
- Creative
- Curious
- Daring
- Demanding
- Disagreeable
- Dreamer
- Energetic
- Excited
- Fancy
- Friendly
- Fun-loving
- Funny
- Happy

- Helpful
- Humorous
- Impulsive
- Intelligent
- Inventive
- Keen
- Lazy
- Lovable
- Pitiful
- Plain
- Pleasing
- Proud
- Quiet
- Reserved
- Sad
- Serious
- Shy
- Simple
- Simple-minded
- Smart
- Studious
- Thoughtful
- Thrilling
- Timid
- Witty

Respect

Do you have a friend who seems to command instant respect in almost any situation?

How do they do it and what is their secret?

They treat themselves well, and other's sense it and go along with it. Respect yourself and others will often respect you too. Hold firm with your beliefs with confidence and others will respect your strength of character. Remember to carry yourself tall and "Dress your best," physically and mentally, even when you don't quite feel it.

Respect and take control of your personal spaces and treat them well. Your home should reflect someone who is in control. If it is a cluttered mess, what is that saying about your internal world?

Respect your clothing and everything you own. If you don't respect the items in your possession, if they just don't hold any value, get rid of them by passing them on to someone who will value them. No matter what your surroundings and where you live, respect yourself and those in your neighbourhood.

Respect has a marked effect on your self-esteem and your life. People with low self-esteem are typically not respecting their basic human rights, their character traits, nor properly respecting those around them. You can only feel genuinely happy when you accept your personal strengths and power. You are living a lie when you are functioning from your perceived weaknesses. Weakness often comes from not asking others for help when you need it. There is a tipping-point in our struggle when we need to reach out for support. It is weak to continue on losing a struggle when others would just seek help. You are likely putting up with things because you don't want to burden others with your troubles. Be strong and ask!

Why realists can struggle with happiness and positivity

When you ask people if they see themselves as positive, most people will say they are. If you ask people if they think they are negative, the response you will get is that they are being realistic about life. What does being realistic mean?

Well, unless you can read the future, realism means forming your first opinion from your own past interpreted experiences and predicting what might happen in the future. Realists take their second opinion from tv, films, books or those in the position of authority. Realistic people will either take an optimistic view or a pessimistic view and some will take both views at the same time. An optimistic or pessimistic view is a reflection of the state of your self-esteem. Realistic people try and predict the future, dealing with views and opinions which often do not equate to future realities and expected consequences.

If I ask 20 people to give me their realistic view on what colour tomorrow's dawn will be, I will get a number of answers, all depending on their own unique perspective and where their source of evidence has come from. It is very difficult to be realistic and right when we carry around personal biases and cherry-pick evidence for that of which we cannot be certain. Politicians always come across as certain because their jobs and reputations are on the line. They will prove things by twisting their original statements and cherry-picking their evidence after the event has happened, through the benefit of hindsight. Well, we can all win when we use hindsight as our evidence. It is like winning the lottery by selecting your numbers after they are drawn.

The traditional realists we know look to the past and predict the future. Remember that we only control our feelings and reactions to external events in this moment. We cannot do anything about the past except forget about it and move on, learn from it, or change our opinion of it. We can only influence and inspire change for the future by what we do in this moment. Realism, as a happy and positive person would define it, is living this moment to the next with an optimistic feeling. Nothing more, nothing less.

The affect of authority figures on our self-esteem

Authority figures in your life have likely had a powerful impact on how your happiness and self-esteem has been shaped. Many of us, as children, grew up with worried parents who taught us how to be anxious and worried. They modelled this behaviour in front of our eyes. They mostly controlled what we owned, what we ate, which friends we saw and the activities we participated in. This was done through their parental instinct of keeping us safe and protected. As a result, we learned that so many things can be dangerous in our world and that we should be very careful, particularly of taking risks. If a child came from a home where they were neglected or abused, their parental figures modelled this behaviour as normal treatment, which as responsible adults we know as not normal.

As we grew, further authority figures influence our impressionable minds: teachers, police, peers we admired, celebrities and heroes. As we matured still: Politicians and Religious figures, Company CEO's and managers. Every single person we have met in the world has had the opportunity to influence us and shape our self-esteem in a good or bad way. That is why it is important for you to now define your values, beliefs and thoughts as your own with a new positive and happy filter.

When you continue to entertain negative thinking, know that your negative thoughts come in packs. As like attracts like, when you start with one negative thought, it will attract another until they occupy much of your thinking. This is why it is important to not entertain a single negative thinking and challenge it as soon as you are aware. If you like playing the victim for other's sympathy, negative thoughts will serve you well in the short term; however, you will never be independent if your self-worth relies on other people's attention out of sympathy.

How one negative thought leads to another

1. Your manager raises their voice at you in work and you think, "Why is she being horrible to me?"
2. "Why doesn't she like me?"
3. "Why do I have to work in such a horrible place?"
4. "It's not worth the money I'm paid!"
5. "I'm better off not working here and getting a job somewhere else. Maybe they'll appreciate me more."
6. "I get up so early to be here and work so late, yet no one seems to notice my sacrifice."
7. "I would love to tell my boss where to stick it!"
8. "If I won the lottery...!"

9. "Imagine if I inherited a fortune from a lost relative."

And the fantasies of leaving your work for some incredible fortune or for enacting revenge, continue to play out in your mind, while nothing actually changes.

Exercise 10: Reframing Negative thoughts

When your first negative thought comes up, catch it quickly and reframe it!

Try this simple visualisation. Imagine a drab brown picture frame around a beautiful masterpiece like one of Vincent van Gogh's sunflower paintings. Notice how the drabness drains the bright, warm colours from the painting. Now imagine placing a lustrous, yellow-gold frame around the painting. It will bring out the beautiful colours of the sunflower and put the painting into a new, glowing light.

We can imaginatively use the technique of reframing a picture to change the feeling of a negative image that is troubling our mind.

Consider the first thought in the previous work scenario, "Why is she being horrible to me?"

We can use different frames of reason for the manager's behaviour that reframes our initial assumed judgement,

- "Maybe she is stressed by something else!"
- "Maybe her boss had a go at her!"

We can also use simple humour frames:

- "We all have our bad days, and this looks like a doozy for her."
- "Someone got up on the wrong side of bed this morning."

While humour can quite quickly disarm anger and anxiety, it

doesn't have to be at someone else's expense. You can also follow up with a line of compassion:

- "We all have our bad days, and this looks like a doozy for her. I'll ask her if everything is okay when she seems more relaxed."
- "Someone got up on the wrong side of bed this morning. I'll sort this out and then let her know, it may take the stress off."

Take a troubling image that continues to be stuck in your mind and try the following:

- Imagine turning the scene into a picture and putting a candy-striped frame around it. How does this make you feel?
- Imagine playing silly music and dressing everyone in a silly costume and laughing.
- Imagine shrinking the image into nothing.
- Imagine screwing up the image into a ball and then tossing it in a bin.
- Imagine turning the image into a painting and throwing water over it and then watching the colours run out of it until it is a blank canvas.
- Imagine putting the image into an imaginary shredder and shredding it into confetti.
- If you are continuously replaying a troubling scene as if it were a movie, imagine rewinding it quickly and seeing your manager moving backwards at a fast and funny pace or fast-forwarding it from beginning to end with all the action in fast forward.
- If you are hearing your own negative voice or another's negative voice in your mind, try making the comments squeaky like Mickey Mouse, or making them deep and slow, or in the voice of the Wicked Witch of the West.

The purpose of the above exercises are to take out the power from the negative feeling experienced in the situation and replace it with a positive, humorous and lighter view. Therefore, when you re-visit the image or re-play the scene, you are likely to have a newly conditioned, reframed positive reaction to the event.

If you are really unhappy with a situation and want to take action, you want to focus on your known personal strengths and speak with the concerned party in a mature and respectful way. Always:

- Keep calm and supportive
- Let them know how you have been affected by the situation
- Offer solutions and not more problems
- State factual observations

You can ask them for ways to improve the situation or offer them ways on how you can improve the situation; however, demonstrate that you are being supportive and proactive:

"I've been noticing that you have been raising your voice at me the past few days and I want you to know that this has worried me. Can we discuss exactly what you are upset about so I know if I can improve the situation or whether there is a way I can support you better in future?

Like attracts like whether it be positive or negative.

Negative thinking is like junk food. It presents as a fast and easy option to just complain about something and then wash your hands of doing anything about it. You make no effort for changing the situation and instead putting the onus of responsibility on others or events. Just like fast food, blaming has no substance and is not at all nutritious for anyone's wellbeing. It is addictive and may give momentary pleasure if there's an audience to complain to; but in the long-run, the stress of negative thoughts accumulates. When you are addicted to negative thinking, you are fighting a losing battle as negative feelings relate to things beyond your control.

We know when eating healthily, what we put in our mouths is vital for our health. Well, the same goes for what we put in our minds!

There is a well-established principal in computer programming abbreviated as GIGO; it stands for,

"Garbage in, garbage out"

Just like a computer, your unconscious mind cannot discern the bad data from the good and will take it all in to make an impression of an event. That is not good news for those who continue negative thinking throughout their lives. Thinking it will improve them in some way or believing they are being realistic about things is just not logical.

HERE IS some of the garbage we might fill our minds with:

- "I'm useless!"
- "I hate my life!"
- "Why is everything so hard!"
- "If I was only more like ......!"
- "Nothing's fair!"
- "Why is everybody so unkind!"

Notice the generalisations used in these junk statements: "everything," "nothing," "everybody."

The quickest way to take the power out of a generalisation is to add a question mark and repeat the generalisation in a challenging question:

- "Everything is hard?"

- "Nothing is fair?"
- "Everybody is unkind?"

I REMEMBER when growing up in Australia my friends often used to say the same message over and over, which stuck in my mind for many years:

"LIFE IS shit and then you die!"

I HAD to change and reframe that message as it came up so frequently when I faced challenges, so I changed it to,

"LIFE IS GREAT, and I choose my fate!"

IT BECAME an automatic mantra every time the other phrase came into my mind, and it still does as I write this!

JUST AS EATING healthy food takes some practice, so too does not allowing a garbage thought to occupy your mind. You have to consciously catch it and reframe into a positive thought. After a while, you will find yourself automatically challenging negative statements as a matter of habit.

Knowing the rules of positive thinking and having an optimistic view of the world will promote happiness in your life. You need to start by consciously challenging your viewpoint. The quickest way to becoming a victim is by seeing life in a negative way, and I've heard some real negatives about life from clients:

- "Life isn't fair!"
- "Life is cruel!"
- "My life is messy!"

Change the words that you use to describe life and give the following a read through:

- "Life is sweet!"
- "Life is an adventure!"
- "Life is the colours of a rainbow!"
- "Life is a garden of flowers!"
- "Life is a game!"

THE PURSUIT of leading a positive life can be fun. Imagine a Monopoly board and choose the piece that you wish to be the vehicle to transport you through life.

The Scottie dog
The hat
The thimble
The boot
The wheelbarrow
The cat
The racing car
The battleship
And in the older version of the game:
The iron
The rocking horse
The lantern
The horse and rider
The sack of money

.   .   .

PERSONALLY, I've always been drawn to the horse which in my mind symbolises strength and sensitivity combined. I don't particularly wish to be in a wheelbarrow and having another take control of my ride! How you choose to travel through your life in will determine your experiences and the obstacles you encounter.

Taking it to heart

As thoughts always come before a feeling, what happens in your head, also moves to your heart. If you want happiness, your thoughts must support that feeling.

We all have negative thoughts no matter who we are; however, do you want more negative thoughts or less, because it is the amount that makes the difference? The average number of thoughts a person has in a day is in the thousands. Imagine thousands of negative thoughts! What must that do to your thinking?

Now imagine thousands of positive thoughts!

Dream about the good things and you will attract more of them. Have constant nightmares of the bad and you will start living them as you project them from your inside world to your outside world. This is because our world is a mirror of our self-esteem. What you feel, is what you project. If you have ever heard the old expression "Wearing your heart on your sleeve," this is exactly what we are talking about. If you feel suspicious or cautious, you will appear unapproachable. If you feel positive and welcoming, you will appear more approachable. If you feel too cool for school, you might freeze everybody out. No matter how many designer clothes you wear, the plastic surgery you may have undertaken, the weight loss, the muscle building, if you are miserable on the inside, you have to change that first!

Changing your environment, changing your car, changing your job, changing your house, changing your partner are expensive solutions to just choosing to change yourself first. Material changes are a distraction for what really needs to be changed in order to be happy more often.

Happy self-esteem

There is a sensible and realistic way of living a friendly, positive and optimistic life where you project self-confidence and still maintain your happy outlook. This is what you need to keep in check:

- Know your life is about you first, it is not to be controlled by other people even your closest family and friends.
- If you feel like you have to please everyone, expect that someone will try and take advantage. Knowing you are worthwhile and deserve better treatment, and just don't give in to them.
- If the people around you enjoy treating you badly, stand up to them in an open and respectful way or seek the appropriate support to deal with them.
- Associate with supportive people for your close circle of friends. You do not have to remain in degrading relationships where your confidence and esteem is constantly under criticism.
- Lead your own life and don't sacrifice it to live to another's agenda.
- Value your own worth, value your time, value your knowledge, value your opinions and value your aspirations, and then choose to attend to other's who are not using you or imposing on your time.
- Remember, if you don't make choices, others will make them for you.

Accept your right to be assertive with yourself and others and give

- Do you deserve to be paid peanuts?
- Do you deserve to be shouted at?
- Do you deserve to be the butt of other's jokes?

- Do other people deserve to be given the best from you if you choose to give it?

Accept yourself and you will start to be accepted by others because you will project a state of acceptance to others. Love yourself and people will love you because you give love. Do not be afraid of giving from your positive feelings inside. Love is a gift to give, encouragement is a gift to give, respect is also a gift to give. It is nothing to be embarrassed about, and if you don't do it now, you may regret having not given later in your life. You are not cool or more respectful for holding all this good energy inside of yourself.

What is reflected back to you in your life are messages of how you are living it. If mostly good things are happening, life is telling you that your thoughts and feelings are working for you. If bad things are happening, you are getting a call from your unconscious that something about you needs to change for the positive. Identifying and making this change will improve your self-esteem!

The Pros and Cons

There is a well-known and well-used saying that,

"When the student is ready, the teacher will appear."

Many of us seek the one person who will guide us to a brighter future; a teacher and role-model who will show us the way. As children, teenagers and young adults, teachers and mentors make a huge impact in shaping us. Many teachers do not even realise the impact they have upon us. However, it will come to the point as you grow older when you know the best teacher is yourself. Self-learning builds your resilience, your self-reliance and your self-esteem.

There are plenty of digital sources available at our fingertips to learn pretty much anything in our world. Adult learning teachers and mentors act more as coaches these days, who help you refine and put into practice the information you have absorbed through self-study.

No longer do you need to seek gurus for your enlightenment when many of the great teachers can be watched online. The teacher does not need to appear, they are already inside you and in front of you. The greatest teacher of all is experience, and experience comes from practical trial and error. Rather than wait for a teacher, just get on and start having a go in even the smallest of ways.

The balance of probabilities

When you feel optimistic and happy, and you visualise the people that you want in your life, you will start to attract these people in your life; the right partner, the right friends, colleagues, and coaches. You will attract the right opportunities because you will start to recognise more opportunities. Soon any pros will outweigh any cons as you become a positive pro at managing the cons. If you see the world negatively, every opportunity will have more cons as you become condescendingly critical of any pros.

Always emphasise the positive results no matter how small they are and persist in your practice of optimism and happiness. In the light of newly-found optimism, your inner-critic will get the idea and start to leave you alone.

Imagine an old-fashioned weighing scale with two plates at either end of a balancing arm. The balance of probabilities says that by having more positive thoughts, one side of the scale will tip you toward happiness, while more negatives on one side will tip you toward unhappiness.

The comparison trap

With low self-esteem, the tendency is to fall into a habitual comparison trap:

- "I look better than her, don't I?"
- "I wish I looked more like her."
- "If I was just like him, then I would be more successful."

We cannot be all things to all people and why do we have to please anybody anyway? a need to please other people through your appearance or actions is a sign of a troubling self-esteem. You are spending your life to impress or please with no guarantees.

ROMAN STOIC MARCUS AURELIUS said that we must,
   "stand erect, not be kept erect by others."

IF YOU STILL FIND YOU have the habit of comparing yourselves to others, a solution lies in what many spiritual groups have practiced over the centuries. It is the process of forgiving ourselves for our faults and recognising that we are imperfect and that is okay.

It is called self-compassion, and when you have self-compassion, you put comparison to a complete halt.

Rather than looking for the differences between us and everyone we scrutinise, look instead for the similarities, and it is there that you will find connection. There is:

- no "better"
- no "different"
- no "luckier"
- no "happier"

THESE ARE subjective words that differ from one person to the next. Our similarities are the everyday aspects of our shared humanity. As one of my University colleagues said quite succinctly,

"NO MATTER WHO YOU ARE, we all p*ss and sh*t!"

. . .

WITH THIS FOCUS on similarities and not differences, there is less need to compete with others and more need to compete with ourselves. We all want to improve, but improving is our responsibility, not the responsibility of others who can only advise us on how to improve.

When it comes to self-esteem, accept yourself and feel good and you will attract better experiences. Criticise yourself and feel bad and you will attract even worse experiences. It is simply a balance of probabilities.

5

RESILIENCE IN THE FACE OF RESISTANCE

KEEP ON KEEPING ON (WITH A SMILE INSIDE)

F ear, loss, hurt, disappointment and failing are all a part of our lives. They can cause us temporary setbacks as we rebuild our composure to face life again.

A setback need only occur for the time it takes to get our thinking straight again; that is, reframing negative thoughts to positive thoughts and then moving forward again. Feelings are an expression of our interpretation of an event. The event isn't necessarily the cause of how you feel, but the sense of loss that comes from it. We all respond differently to loss and bounce back at different rates.

- You react with disappointment when you don't win that competition.
- *You have lost a dream option that you may have been counting on.*
- You react with anger when that person cuts in front of you in their car.
- *You have lost your pride as you feel someone has disrespected you personally or hasn't followed the rules of the road.*

Often we find ourself stuck in a cycle of emotions as we keep thinking about a loss in our lives. How do we break out of that cycle?

When you study a script as an actor, you look for the subtext or motivation suggested by the lines. You think of the real meaning hidden behind the text so that you can deliver that message in your actions as an actor to create an authentic performance. We need to explore the unconscious motivation behind our own reactions. The unconscious mind is there to protect our survival by providing us with a message for what needs to change. It has the positive intention of improving things for us expressed through what we say and the behaviours we enact. If you are trying to find the reason behind your negative thoughts or actions, keep asking,

- "What's behind that?"

Until you get to a point where an action you can take is under your full control.

Example:

- I get short-tempered when I'm asked a question at work.
- "What's behind, me being short-tempered?"
- I haven't been getting much sleep, so I'm not thinking clearly.
- "What's behind, me not sleeping?"
- I'm finding work stressful and having difficulty sleeping as I keep thinking about problems.
- "What's behind, me having problems and being stressed?"
- I'm not being supported by my manager to get everything done.
- "What's behind, me not feeling supported?"
- I haven't told my manager of the difficulty as I worry that they will think I am not capable enough at my job.
- "What's behind, me feeling I am not capable enough?"
- I feel I don't know how to prioritise all these tasks more efficiently.

If you keep peeling back the layers, you will find an area that is in your control and you can work on and improve. If you find an area is totally out of your control, only address what you can influence or what you can inspire change for.

Exercise 11: What's Behind That?

1. Choose a specific situation where you would like to explore and take control of a negative feeling that is troubling you; e.g. "I feel unappreciated because my manager won't give me more responsibility in my role."
2. Ask yourself, "What's behind, me feeling...?" e.g. "What's behind, me not feeling appreciated?"
3. Note the reply and ensure that you have identified a feeling to address, e.g. "I don't feel that I am fully trusted in my role." Then ask again "What's behind, me not feeling fully trusted?"; e.g. "I didn't get a couple of important projects completed by their deadlines and I think my abilities are being doubted."
4. Continue until you have returned to a point where you can control an action or take further actions to solve the initial problem; e.g. "I am of value to the company and I will ensure I complete every task set by my manager, on time and without complaint, to re-establish trust in my work ethic."

BY TAKING action in reaction to events, you are developing your resilience and advancing your position toward better control, positive experiences and more happiness. When you bow down to events and let them take over your thinking, you lose personal control and experience being powerless or helpless. By viewing the results of events constructively, you will have something to work your way out of any problem.

DISAPPOINTMENT IS the feeling that you didn't give your best effort or that something or someone didn't meet your expectations.

Failing and making mistakes is a part of growing. Making mistakes is an experience that all human beings share. Constructively learning from mistakes improves our path to future success. We also learn from mistakes by observing or learning from the mistakes of others. People who continually improve do so by building a tolerance to the frustration of their needs not being satisfied. As their resilience to setbacks and criticism increases, being happy and positive becomes easier.

Those who give up on challenges quickly develop a lower tolerance to frustration and less resilience as they struggle to meet the early challenges. It is more difficult for them to bounce back in the face of fear or adversity.

What we can learn from Children

Nearly 40 years ago, American psychologist Dr Carol Dweck and her associates became interested in how pupils reacted to failure. They observed that while some pupils rebounded quickly, others were crushed by the smallest of setbacks. Doctor Dweck went on to study hundreds of children and their resilience to setbacks. She formed the model of the 'fixed mindset' and 'growth mindset' to describe the underlying beliefs people have about learning and intelligence. When students operate from a 'fixed mindset,' they have limits to how much they will achieve unless they are taught how to be capable of more. Being taught better capability and better responses to challenges, contributes to forming a 'growth mindset'. When pupils have a 'growth mindset,' they believe that by being responsible and putting in the extra time and effort, they will progress and achieve at a higher level.

Effort and Persistence

To develop a 'growth mindset' you must see the possibilities and the proof around you that 'success' is the reward of persisting in your effort to push yourself beyond your 'comfort zone.' A low tolerance to perceived pain, failure or disappointment are the main obstacles to achievement.

Think back to the very first chapter when you rated obstacles to your happiness out of 10. Some people are devastated by any criticism which, for them, may rank as an 8 out of 10 on the pain threshold. For others, the same criticism may rank as a 3 out of 10 which eventually motivates them to learn from the experience and improve their performance, and then move on.

If your frustration tolerance levels are low, you can see why you would find the events of life extremely challenging. Your personal sense of pride and honour, or your reliance on the outside world to define you, is completely distorted. You are prone to pleasing others and receiving their feedback to boost your self-esteem. On the scales of probability, you would be quickly weighed down by negative feelings at the slightest instance of criticism.

IT IS important that we desensitise our emotional responses to setbacks. If you have an optimistic outlook and refuse to take things too seriously, you will experience more happy moments in life and also attract greater success in your pursuits, knowing that your efforts in the moment are motivated by your positive thoughts of a better future.

If you have low frustration tolerance and a negative outlook on life, happiness will be a rarer experience and you will likely blame external events for your lack.

Ask yourself,

- Do you want your next year to be the same as the one just passed?

- Do you want to be in the same position you are in now in five or ten years in time?

Don't shoot the messenger

Next time you are upset with someone else, know that it's mainly your thoughts about them that are upsetting you, they are not meeting your expectations. They are reflecting a message of what you need to personally improve. If you don't change your approach or your attitudes to even the most difficult of people, you will continue being a victim.

If you have runaway emotional reactions, get too attached to people and their opinions of you, you are in for a world of disappointment, frustration and pain! Don't get angry, don't cry, and don't respond intensely. Instead, consciously turn down the level of these very same feelings to feeling slightly annoyed and slightly disappointed. Then let the other person know how you feel. You can even say something along the lines of,

"I have to let you know that I am a bit put out by this."

"I find this situation a step backwards in communicating properly."

"I need time to reflect before I respond. Let's discuss this tomorrow."

You can even use slightly humorous words to break the tension and defuse the emotions, if it is appropriate.

CHANGE "I FEEL ANGRY!" to:

"I feel vexed!"

"I feel exasperated!"

"I feel irked!"

"I feel piqued!"

CHANGE "I FEEL UPSET/HURT/SAD" to:

"I feel perturbed."

"I feel discombobulated."

"I feel unsettled."

"I feel disconcerted."

IN SITUATIONS where others are upset in your company, do your best to remain open, warm, supportive and encouraging.

Exercise 12: Reacting from a Positive Position

How would you prefer to react when other people project their negative emotions upon you?

This is a very simple exercise but requires you to practice it often, particularly before moments when you think you will need it. It is designed to help you desensitise to difficult situations and emotions. It is also worth practicing after an event has occurred and you did not react the way you would have liked. It can be a cathartic approach in retrospect as it gets out all the negative feelings and gives you a preferred future ability to respond.

1. Choose the positive feeling or feelings you wish to express when faced with a difficult reaction from another person. You may wish to be calm, logical, warm, understanding, empathetic, or assertive.
2. Imagine the situation in your mind and ensure that you see yourself and the people involved at a distance, a dissociated viewpoint.
3. Imagine that the person or people are unleashing their negative emotions on you and what they are saying. Don't respond, just listen.
4. See yourself reacting with your new feelings and how effective these feelings are for helping you to remain balanced.
5. Now amplify the positive sensation of these feelings inside

you and your determination to use them. Let them fill your mind and body, and feel good about them.

6. Replay the scene through an associated viewpoint, this means looking through your own eyes.

7. Imagine the other person or people going through the motions of their actions while you remain strong inside with your new feelings. Their overreaction of emotions wash over you like water off a duck's back. You know that you are in an empowered position with your new, positive feelings.

8. Feel your new feelings deep inside and notice how the other person or people's emotions begin to subside with time.

9. Play through the scene or a slightly different version of the scene as many times as you need while keeping a hold on your desired emotional reactions and responses.

10. Feel empowered that you faced a situation which would normally have unbalanced your emotions, and that you can do the same in a real life. Remember that the unconscious mind has difficulty differentiating what is imaginary from what is real, and this works to your advantage.

Resilience in the face of aggression

"Beware that, when fighting monsters, you yourself do not become a monster. And when you gaze long into the abyss. The abyss gazes also into you."
Friedrich W. Nietzsche

AN AGGRESSIVELY ANGRY person will have difficulty calming down and if you can't escape them or they refuse to leave, you must not confront them unless you are prepared for the possible verbal or physical consequences of their anger. To help maintain your composure when faced with an angry and aggressive person, , use the following tactics to positively deal with the event as best you can:

- Remain quiet, calm and attentive.
- Listen and don't interrupt their outburst.
- Do not correct them.
- Do not make any excuses.
- Admit any obvious errors on your part or the part of the organisation you work for, and offer reasonable help if you can do so.
- Show them you are doing your best, don't tell them as they will say you are not.
- Give them a timeframe when a helpful starting action will be completed.
- Let them know how you will follow up and how you will contact them in the very near future. Make sure that you do.

Challenge is inevitable

Life will always present challenges and you will always have to adapt to meet them, right up until your last dying day. If you have a 'fixed mindset' of your capabilities, life will seem cruel and out to get you. If you have a 'growth mindset' you will fill your life with learning new skills, strategies and tactics to continue meeting the challenges that life presents.

In William Ernest Henley's poem "Invictus" about the dignity of courage in life and facing death, his last stanza concludes with a stirring statement for responsibility:

IT MATTERS NOT how strait the gate,
　　How charged with punishments the scroll,
　　I am the master of my fate,
　　I am the Captain of my soul.

. . .

IN OTHER WORDS, you solely have control over determining your feelings and your destiny despite the obstacles in life.

Any obstacle can be dealt with in one way or another. Like a Captain in charge of your own self, you can utilise your 'growth mindset' and figuratively take any of the following actions when facing an obstacle:

1. Outrank it with your knowledge and confidence, and take charge of the situation.
2. Outflank it by finding a weaknesses in the obstacle and break it down bit-by-bit.
3. Completely avoid it by finding another path around it.

If you approach the obstacle with a 'fixed mindset' you will most likely:

- Surrender to it.
- Retreat.

THE CHILDREN'S book "We're Going on a Bear Hunt" written by Michael Rosen and illustrated by Helen Oxenbury, is a story of bravery, resilience and humour. It is about two parents and their three children on an adventurous journey to find a bear. As they travel, they meet many natural obstacles, and the refrain follows the following pattern:

"UH-UH A RIVER
 A Deep cold river
 We can't go over it
 We can't go under it

Oh no! We've got to go through it!"

AND THAT IS EXACTLY what they do, right up until they meet the bear in a dark cave and run back through all the obstacles in a panic. The obstacles were such an issue when they were on their adventure, but they quickly travel through them in the face of a larger threat following behind them.

WHEN FACING a challenge that you have doubts about start by simply saying to yourself,

- "I can do this!" or if it is more challenging,
- "If others can do this, there is no reason why I can't give it a good go too!"

On occasions, my Dad said the following to me when I wasn't sure of my abilities,

- "If they can do it, you can do it too! That is, if you really want it."

OF COURSE, environment, opportunity and chance have an impact on the level of difficulty you may face. However, these can not be used as excuses for an individual not to take responsibility for making things happen while avoiding challenge. Excuses are excuses. Others have found their way out of poverty or lack, and others have worked to improve the poverty or lack around them.

Self-reliance in learning and improving

When you want to make a change, always begin with yourself first. You need to take the initiative and then be persistent in consciously managing your thoughts and actions. Persistency and consistency are practices you must embrace in order to incrementally improve. Do the study you need to do to make the improvements. Seek the situations you need to experience to make the improvements.

Information and instruction are so readily available on the internet now, and free. Take the actions you need to take. Inaction will get you nowhere and will be the difference between you improving or not improving. We should no longer be looking at the outside world as responsible for our happiness and growth.

As your first response to events, take responsibility for your feelings and actions, don't blame external events or people for your choice to not take action. You may feel hindered by outside forces effecting your position in life but the work to make a change always comes from you. Take the initiative and ask yourself,

- Who am I making this change for? To impress someone else or to be my best self?
- Who really will make me become my best self?

Resilience overrides procrastination caused by fear

People who do little with their lives are just as fearful as people who take massive risks. The difference is that the first group are fearful of the smallest things and they end up paralysed with inaction or distraction, whereas the second group have a sense that most things will work out okay and they will learn on the way. Why not get scared over something much larger than the little things that bother you?

If little things become big obstacles for you, then you are still placing too much emphasis on the feedback you might get from the outside world. The little things are just little things of very little importance and there is no need to fear them. Often, many of the obstacles we perceive as bigger things are just little things too.

Will you remember them tomorrow, next week, or next year?

Are they newsworthy events?

Growth is most painful when we resist it, and resistance often triggers procrastination. Put off something for long enough and it starts to consume your mind, causing you pain and anxiety. Get on and do it and you will find relief and realise it was not worth putting off in the first place. Consequences grow for things we do not take responsibility for. Rise to these challenges, like the responsible and strong person you deserve to be. As a happy and positive person, things lose their annoyance factor by taking action. You have learned not to put off short-term inconveniences. Instead, you strive for the rewards of long-term pleasure by completing any short-term inconveniences before they grow into problems.

If in doubt about whether to do it now or later, just do it now anyway. It will be one less thing to tackle later. You no longer have to deal with a problem if you no longer have a problem to deal with.

Carrying unecessary burdens

If you can no longer bear the weight of something that you consider to be a burden, quit wasting your thoughts on it and learn to let it go. You cannot be happy when you are constantly worried about the weight you carry on your shoulders, especially if you are bothering other people by talking about it all the time. Drop it! You care for yourself best carrying only what serves you well. Good things are light in weight and negative things weigh you down with the heft of the associated stress. Unload the weight and you will feel lighter. When you lighten the load, the relief creates feelings of excitement for a more positive future and inspires you to continue making further positive changes. You will be happier and find that others will be curious or inspired by your change in nature.

The excitement of relief and feeling lighter is a much better state to share with your family and friends than burdening them with your worry or anxiety. Good family and friends want you to feel happy. There is no need to appear desperate or concerned all the time, that reflects a weakness in your integrity. Very successful people detach from the woes of life and focus instead on the excitement of a new challenge. They do not care so much about lining up all their little ducks in a row; as long as they are travelling the right stream, all is well.

Exercise 13: Letting go of your Burdens

Most of our burdens come from the roles we play in our lives. To help yourself lighten your load, answer the following questions:

What unwanted burdens do you carry in your role as a:

- Healthy person
- Employee
- Manager
- Leader
- Advisor/Counsellor
- Parent
- Grandparent
- Child
- Role-model
- Learner
- Teacher
- Team-mate
- Performer
- Partner
- Lover

If you wish to relieve yourself from the weight of the burdens you carry, begin with what weighs heavily on your mind and use the following imaginative exercise:

1. Close you eyes.

2. Imagine your burdens as physical representations, e.g. guilt over disappointing someone as a large hat on your head, fear of speaking to other people as a long scarf around your neck, and your shame of a past addiction as a heavy rucksack on your back.

3. See yourself walking along and feeling the weight of all the burdens you carry and how they are slowing you down.

4. As you walk along, stop every now and shed one of the burdens. You might put it in a bin or recycling unit, burn it in a fire or incinerator or atomise it with a laser.

5. As you begin walking again, notice how much faster you move and how much lighter you feel every time you offload one of the burdens until they are all released.

6. Practice this exercise each day until you feel you have lightened your load significantly. Every time you practice, you will notice that there is no real reason for you to hold onto these once troubling burdens anymore.

Instant preparation for facing an obstacle

What is most important in your life is not the possessions that you own but the feelings that you have on a regular basis. People wish to possess certain objects or achieve certain goals to feel a desired feeling; such as, security, safety, happiness, feeling special, powerful or having a sense of self-assuredness. This is a backwards approach to getting what you could just have right now.

When dreaming of something you want to attain, don't just wish for it, imagine you already have it. Then extract the feelings, attitudes and beliefs behind possessing this object or achievement.

WHAT DO I want to feel by owning this?

What do I want to feel by achieving this?

·   ·   ·

IMAGINE these feelings now to meet the obstacles on your path to actually possessing or achieving this desire. These feelings are likely the exact same that a successful person in your desired field would perform from in their everyday life. It may be a quiet confidence, certainty, or an extroverted warmth and friendliness. You can choose to act from these feelings without the years it has taken another to discover them. Don't feel that you have to "earn" feelings because that makes no sense. Feelings are states, they ebb and flow naturally, no matter who you are and what you have done. With conscious practice, you can evoke them yourself by thinking positively, imaging having them in situations where you would like to utilise them and physically holding yourself upright and in a strong but relaxed manner.

There is nothing mystical about feelings. We do not need a guru to lead us to experiencing them. We are talking about feelings which most of the population has already experienced and does not take any time to develop. If you can behave in a morose, angry, frustrated or anxious way, then you can choose to behave in any positive way that you need to help move you toward your dreams. It beats choosing to be under-confident and disbelieving your own worth.

High standards, low expectations

Roman Stoic Marcus Aurelius said,

"Be tolerant with others but strict with yourself."

RAISE your standards for yourself but lower your expectations of others so you will not be disappointed by their behaviour. You can choose to give your best because you are in control of your best; you can't expect others to give their best as you cannot control their behaviour.

You can raise your standards to be the strongest link in your chain of relationships, you are the most resilient, and you are in control of your own reactions. When you fight against others and their expectations, or if you rail against the world and what is happening, you have a low chance of winning. It is important that you protect your beliefs and standards by operating from your attitudes and reactions; however, do not expect to change others very easily.

Being resilient one step at a time

Every event in life can transform us, give us insight or make us stronger. Catastrophes will likely have the biggest impact on our thoughts and beliefs. Take the events negatively and you have a very large pit of despair to climb out of. Seek something positive and transformative and you will help yourself and others to overcome almost any disaster.

This is what resilience is all about. When you've been floored by a life event, look for that glimmer of survival and let it grow. When you are on your knees, say to yourself: "I'm fed up with being broke! I'm fed up with being pushed around! I'm fed up with being unhappy!" When you are utterly fed up with something, you will seek a way to improve your situation.

WHEN THE GOING GETS TOUGH, the tough get going.

WHEN YOU ARE on the ropes, to improve your situation you have to dig deep:

- Know that you are the only one who can ultimately help yourself in every experience you encounter. Reaching out to ask for advice or guidance from others is also helping yourself.
- Do anything to improve yourself and your situation, no matter how small the action that you take.
- Know that you can't control what is outside of yourself,

you can only inspire change by acting as a role-model for change.

IN AN EXTREMELY TOUGH CIRCUMSTANCE, look for that glimmer of light and keep moving forward, reminding yourself at every step:

- "What is my goal/objective/target?" no matter how small the step.
- "I am not yet dead, keep going!"
- "Just one more ...."
- "I can do this!"

WORK THROUGH THE CHALLENGING EXPERIENCE, conquer it, then leave it behind you. If you are broke, alone, in trouble, devastated or at your lowest, you challenge your problems one step at a time and in that moment. You move and act moment-by-moment as you would walking through the deepest of mud, climbing a cliff face, crossing a wilderness. You don't look back, you occasionally look forward to the objective, but you spend most of your time on the action of moving. All your effort goes into your next step until your objective is met.

Each step that you take reflects your resilience until eventually you find that the worst is over. Things will pass and then get better.

The Human Condition

Many happy people have overcome serious set-backs in life. It is part of our condition as a human that we will face many of the same events in life. The "Human Condition" accounts for the essential milestones of our existence: birth, growth, age, emotions, aspirations, conflict, pain, and death.

In their past, many happy people I have met have been financially broke, emotionally broken, seriously ill, and lost people close to them. Knowing that we all share the conditions of humanity, raise your standards to experience more happiness in life, despite your circumstance. If you can choose to be miserable, then you can choose to be happy and learn to not compromise for anything less; after all, happiness is a part of the "Human Condition" too.

LIKE EVERYONE, happy people have their problems, but the difference is they focus on solutions by looking at the bright-side of a difficulty. They have developed their resilience by choosing to follow a path to its end and have expected to tackle obstacles as they have arisen.

Like a muscle, exercising your problem-solving skills builds resilience, and the struggles you meet, builds your strength to go on.

If you hide indoors watching the world through your television, you might learn a lot of facts about the world, but in no way will you be applying that knowledge until you step out of the front door.

BEING a positive and happy while remaining resilient means you:

- Rise up to risks that are just out of your "comfort zone."
- Rise up when you fail as these are opportunities to learn and improve.
- Rise up and bounce back from criticism and apply it in a constructive to improve your advantage.

WHEN YOU START ANY JOURNEY, you can never be sure of everything ahead, nor how it will end. Your map will only show some of the waypoints, and your journey will require flexibility and adaptability. Start accepting that things may not turn out how you expect because there are simply no guarantees. You might even do better than you originally thought.

The most important thing is to commit and start to write that book, begin that business, get that study done, find and develop that relationship, save that money, build that fitness, and eat more healthy food.

Consistency and persistence

If you really want to make something happen, know that you will need to give it your best go, typically more than just once. It will probably take many mistakes to learn, just like when you learned to write or memorised spelling words. This is how our human world works, through conscious trial and error and continuous and consistent practice.

Many of us have lost touch with the realities of nature. We are fed with instant stories of overnight success from the media, especially social media. In our natural world think how many sperm raced to fertilise the egg that became you. Think of the natural act of attrition where many seeds are sown but only some survive, grow and spread their own seed. Life is a numbers game, and you have to cast your line many times in order to catch a fish. The more you cast your line, the higher your chances. Be prepared to always persist as:

- You are unlikely to get the first and only job you apply for.
- You are unlikely to form a relationship with the first person you go on a date with.
- You are unlikely to sell a product to every person you meet.

The odds are against you, but persistence and effort raise the odds.

WHEN SOMETHING GOES WRONG, there's no point dwelling on it, accept it and react with constructive actions. Raise your levels of resilience by debating strongly with yourself. You must take control of your thoughts and get yourself together in a positive way. If you react from a "growth mindset" you will increase your odds of success and be happier with the results. Be negative and critical and you might as well have just rolled over in defeat with your legs in the air like a submissive puppy. Many misfortunes are opportunities to improve. Take advantage of even a glimmer of an opportunity. Invest in it and it will grow.

Even when life knocks your confidence, start to gather your strength by appreciating good things about yourself; be happy and reassured knowing that things will get better. All things pass for every single one of us and we must enjoy what is good for us until we also come to pass.

Quit while you're ahead but not when you are only just starting

Resilience improves your happiness. It gives you the choice to quit after you have achieved success when you still feel good about your efforts and achievements. This is a far better experience than quitting just after facing your first knock-back and then allowing the negative feelings to cause you to give up.

Success is often more about persistence than talent. It is proving you can go that extra mile. Quitting before the start of the race weakens your tolerance to frustration and stops your chance of a possibly exciting path to travel. Quitting when there is no further improvement to be made is always the best option. After the peak of any achievement, there is always a decline. When you have recognised your peak, look for your next challenge to improve.

Practice and you will improve. Keep practicing and you will improve even more. Practice, practice, and practice some more and you may become an expert. By practicing even with a little consistency, you can know how rewarding something potentially is before you decide to give it up, if you find it just doesn't light your flames of passion to pursue it. Until you've tasted something yourself, you cannot judge whether it is good or bad.

Waining enthusiasm

Have you ever read an inspiring book, been to some motivating training, heard an incredible speech that spoke the truth to you, or been out on a date where you came home on cloud 9? It was a life-changing experience, and gave you a fresh view of the world and all its glories. You felt so optimistic and everything seemed much easier with your new-found energy. Suddenly life was a breeze. Then, everything slowly returned back to how it was before. Normal and slightly dull!

IN THEIR ARTICLE, "Hedonic Relativism and Planning the Good Society" (1971), Social Psychologist, Philip Brickman and Social Scientist, Donald T. Campbell noted that people keep a stable baseline level of happiness despite external events and changes in their fortunes. This behaviour pattern has been labelled the "Hedonic Treadmill" or "Hedonic Adaptation." No matter what exciting or fresh event you experience in life, it eventually becomes the new normal and you return to a relatively comfortable state of being. Wealth, new love, achievements and acquisitions all lose their initial excitement as you shortly return to your normal baseline of happiness. It is like we are forever chasing rainbows or highs.

The people who are able to keep their excitement continuing have one trait in common, they are fascinated by the world around them and find pleasure in appreciating the simple things in life. They are happy to find and explore new experiences and always open to new learning. They keep an optimistic frame of mind and a general state of happiness by:

- Living as much as possible in the moment.
- Appreciating the smallest of experiences.
- Finding beauty and awe in almost anything.
- Continuing to read inspirational books, whether fiction or non-fiction.

- Keeping positive friends.
- Maintaining and deepening their love for their significant other/s.
- Having faith and hope.
- Turning negatives into positives.
- Being resilient and positive in the face of adversity.
- Always having a challenge in their life to keep them moving forward.
- Forgiving their own mistakes and those of others by letting go of what is in the past.

The stretch in resilience

The moment that tests your resilience and when most people typically give up is in the eleventh hour. Things usually look the worst in the eleventh hour, when you only have one or a few more chances left to make a success before you give in. If you keep persisting and holding on through the night, the dawn will eventually break. This last bit of resilience is what you need to see things through to their achievement. As a close friend of mine used to say near the end of one of our exhaustingly long gym sessions,

"I've not been beaten yet! One more go!"

The eleventh hour is the final stretch in our achievement and is resilience in a proactive state.

Desperation is different

Desperation is a different thing altogether. It is a reactive state. This is when we haven't made the effort until the eleventh hour, which is often close to being too late. As a result, you feel stressed, worried, unhappy and regretful for not having taken action sooner. Do any of these sound familiar to you?

- We only make life-changing decisions typically near defeat, despite having many opportunities beforehand.

- We only say, "I love you," when our relationship is in strife.
- We desperately seek money, when we have neglected to plan for the bills we have to pay.
- We start tackling that work-assignment, just hours before it is due.
- We start exercising, only after receiving a serious health warning.

BEING reactive is not the way to live. Take action first, not when it is close to being too late!

6

THE HAPPY ART OF ACTING RESPONSIBLY

YOU ARE THE CAUSE AND THE SOLUTION

Developing the habit of taking action seems difficult for many people as their fear of failure and even success prevents them from taking the very first step. When we fear the discomfort that comes with a change, it can bring us to a halt. Overcoming discomfort is easiest when you focus on taking that very first action only, to start. When you don't take action because you want to know everything before you do anything, consider that:

YOU ONLY NEED TO KNOW,
    What you need to know,
    when you need to know it.
    You don't need to know everything before you start.

PEOPLE WILL LOOK for congruency and integrity in the way that you present yourself. Congruency is seeing that your actions match with your feelings and beliefs. Incongruent people are very easy to see through. They just seem fake. The best way to know what someone believes in is to observe the actions they take in the world. Your actions reveal who you truly are. Talk is cheap and active behaviour is everything.

Those who tell us all about their dreams but take no actions towards them are obviously more interested in keeping the dream a dream as they will not fulfil it in reality. They are likely paralysed by the thought of failure, doubt themselves, don't feel strongly motivated or excited enough, and end up stuck in a limbo of wishful thinking.

Planned actions are the way to increase your congruency and integrity as actions reveal strength. If you save money, work out at the gym, practice optimism, or study hard, you are incrementally building your skills through planned actions each and every day.

Action reflects your thoughts and beliefs and strengthens your self-esteem. Just achieving goals does not achieve happiness, it enhances the feeling of happiness. Happiness is not something you can physically hold onto. You can certainly chooses to feel it and project it to others and it can be quite infectious. Be near happy people and you will likely experience happy feelings.

Sometimes you can feel disappointed when you finally reach a goal because the feelings of achieving it do not necessarily last, we go back to the status quo of feeling normal in a relative space of time. It is the effort and persistence in the pursuit of the goal that increases your knowledge and experience and evokes happy thoughts about the pride of achieving against the odds.

Happiness first

Don't make the mistake of waiting for life to get easier in order for you to be happy. Make the choice of being happy first. This choice relies on you being responsible for your own thoughts and actions as no one else can do this for you. Responsibility is a trait of being a strong and independent person of integrity.

. . .

Choose happiness first, without placing any conditions on it. Eradicate thoughts of,

"When I have ...., I'll be happy!"

No, you won't, not in the long-term anyway. If you feel that you have too many problems to be happy, you are right, because your focus in on your problems.

Wouldn't it be better to tackle your problems from a sense of happiness?

The happiest people may start with many more problems than you do, so how can they be happy most of the time, when you are not?

Happiness is not something you can physically hold. It is a state of emotion or "energy in motion." Many people who I have met who are positive in their outlook and present a happy persona, have had a pretty rough life. They have lost loved ones, money, relationships or have had poor health.

Somewhere along the line they have learned that whatever life has thrown at them, it has been better to choose happiness over despair as you meet challenges faster when you are in a positive state of mind.

Wishing to be happy will not bring you happiness, but by consciously behaving in a positive manner you will connect quickly with these feelings, strengthening your ability to be happier more often. You are rehearsing an emotion you have experienced many times before, making it far easier to reproduce through a better outlook on life.

Initially, happiness involves the responsibility of conscious effort until it becomes an unconscious habit

The best place to begin is always from where you are at in the present moment.

- What feeling are you experiencing in this present moment?
- What would it take for you to feel slightly happy right now?
- What excuse is stopping you from choosing to do this right now?

Like building any muscle, it takes some amount of effort to do the small things you feel a little uncomfortable with or can't be bothered with. However, every little action you take in the face of "I can't be bothered!" is one small step to building your muscle of resilience and effort. Use this muscle to cross the threshold of your low frustration tolerance for discomfort.

If you work on the small, difficult tasks first thing in the morning, you can focus more on what you like doing for the rest of the day. Just make it a habit of getting the tedious tasks out of the way knowing that you can enjoy the desired tasks later. Eat your vegetables before enjoying your dessert; the vegetables are actually better for your growth. Exercise your ability to take action with every little challenge you meet.

Don't invest too much time in trivial tasks

To have a harmonious and happy environment requires knowing your priorities; to be able sort the wheat from the chaff, the important from the trivial. I'm sure you have experienced a meeting or a class where things that were important could have been discussed in 5 minutes, yet the meeting seemed to last for over an hour. Too much time was given to even the tiniest of issues on the agenda. We and others, get caught in the trap where we think that things that are important need to be justified by extending the meeting time or writing a long report. Unfortunately, this lack of efficiency creates resentment in a workplace. Who really likes too much red tape that detracts from the practicalities of the job at hand?

I have found that there are people out there who like to sit on their bottoms all day long and create it.

People will only take trivial agenda items seriously when they feel afraid of the consequences for not paying them attention. A bad manager who can't get their priorities right, will emanate a feeling of threat to others for not treating something as seriously as they do. They will defend even the most trivial and pointless of tasks on their agenda to maintain their ego of importance. No-one wants to work in a culture of threat. A quick way to put things into perspective is to ask,

"On a scale out of 1 to 10, how important is this agenda item really?"

To build something effective you need a system that works. You also need to discard the distractions and the waffle that goes on around you and focus on what is essential. Making a mountain out of a molehill is not healthy for anyone. Systems that work tend to be immediate, action-oriented and brief. If any extra depth is needed, it can simply be added as required through trial and error. Clutter is not only physical, it can be mental as well. By reducing the clutter of your mind, you take the pressure off so that mountains now become molehills.

Action over thoughts and words

You get motivated by taking action and pushing past that first feeling of discomfort. Once you get started, you gain momentum. Taking action is like driving a car; you start by pulling onto the road in first gear. As you gain speed, you change gears. You can't expect a smooth and consistent ride and you occasionally must slow down for other traffic, sometimes coming to a momentary halt because of other obstacles on the road. To get to your dream destination, expect other traffic and stop-starts.

We must always ensure our ownership of the task and our responsibility for our actions overrides any temptation to just do nothing. Nearly everything that has ever happened in our lives has been a result of our own creation through our actions or inactions.

Develop a reputation for yourself as one who is responsible, one who takes action and doesn't put things off. Procrastination and blaming outside sources could bring on unwanted feelings such as guilt, shame and unfounded anger and frustration. Start anywhere you possibly can, even the tiniest action is a move in the right direction. Give your best to whatever task or obstacle is in front of you, and you will begin to develop a habit for being responsible. As a result, more opportunities for learning and achievement will present themselves to you.

Those who speak eloquent words will eventually be caught out if their words do not translate into actions. They are being incongruent in their words and actions.

Too many distractions

There are so many products, beliefs, lifestyles and demands vying for our attention, especially since the advent of digital marketing and social media. This can leave us in a state of not knowing what we want to do and doing nothing. There is just too much temptation and too much choice on offer.

To succeed at anything, you don't need to know everything about it before you start. 'Analysis paralysis' is what keeps many of us stuck, worrying about getting everything right before we have even started. In most cases, people who have succeeded in their field have done so by jumping in and making mistakes, learning invaluable lessons along the way. Having a plan is just like having a map to get to your destination; however, the map is not the territory you traverse, and there will be many changes of direction and adjustments in your course as you forge a path toward your goal.

Know that most people quit, and the true winners are those who persist despite their level of learning, talents and skills. They are like the hero in an adventure novel who begins their tale with undeveloped strengths and a lack of experience. After being compelled to take action in the face of a threat, they fall into the pits that obstruct the path to their goal. Through sheer determination, they pull themselves out of each pit to finally reach their goal at the conclusion of the story. The journey shapes them personally, forcing them to overcome their weaknesses and draw upon their strengths.

Limiting some of the choices on offer

Some things in our lives need to be black and white in order for us to manage the overwhelm of all the responsibilities and choices on offer. The one rule for black and white choices is that they have a positive impact on us without affecting the wellbeing of anyone else. We cannot expect that others will follow the black and white rules we impose upon them unless they serve everybody equally.

An example of a personal black and white rule would be starting to eat more healthily and exercise regularly. One black and white rule might be to adhere to the S.O.S diet acronym; avoid Sugar, Oil and Salt for the health of your heart. You may have a black and white "three strikes you're out" rule for exercise. You will not miss exercising more than two consecutive days during the week or you will forfeit a weekly treat, such as watching a movie.

You give your best effort when you own the responsibility for doing so. You give your best because you want to enjoy the challenge of the journey to the top of that mountain you are climbing. With the success of completing each step, comes feelings of happiness. I'm sure you have felt relieved and even elated when you have accomplished an achievement. It brings a smile to your face, a reflection of a happy feeling inside, and a sense of completion through effort.

We are natural explorers and learners

Humans are built to explore and face new challenges, that is what satisfies our innate drive for discovery, to improve our living conditions. It is a result of our requirements to survive as a species and provide better chances of survival for our genes through our offspring.

You cannot sit about regretting that you should be as successful as someone else when they have devoted their life to their dream, and you have just thought about doing it. However, you can learn from them and follow a similar path to their success to give your life to your dream; that is, if you really want to take the responsibility and actions to achieve it. At the end of the season, when you harvest the crops of your effort and persistence, you will reap what you have sown.

We live in a world of instant results and as a result, our efforts and persistence have weakened. All we see on the media is the finished product in all its perfection, but not the efforts and patience that an individual or group has devoted to its creation.

There is a way that we can take advantage of today's technology. There are many shortcuts and hacks published online for almost every subject out there. There are people all around us offering advice and step-by-step processes for free or a small fee. You can learn almost any musical instrument from beginner to professional online. You can learn a language and hear it spoken correctly. You can learn all levels and specialties of maths. As someone is out there creating content for your benefit and theirs, the possibilities are almost endless. In order to make a living through advertisements and pay per clicks, content creators have to outdo each other with the best instructions in order to earn a living.

There are now thousands of courses available at your fingertips. The world has never had such a vast learning network available to every person in existence who can access the internet.

Despite any learning and instruction, you are still responsible for putting learning into action. For whatever you want to do, practicing every day is the simplest of answers. However, don't expect progress every single day! Anything of worth involves following the "Triple T Theory":

- Things Take Time!

Expect pain and sacrifice with everything you undertake; expect tiredness, boredom, tediousness and toil, but also expect to feel happy at the accomplishment of each challenge you complete:

- Getting fit involves working your body so that it builds strength and aches less as your resilience builds.
- Learning a language involves concentration and frustration to gain eventual fluency.
- Singing correctly involves much vocal technique before you develop the fine muscle control to create the expressive sounds you desire.

Planning long-term achievements over short-term pleasures

When taking action, use your resilience to sacrifice those instant short-term distractions and pleasures to meet your long-term goals. Achieving a long-term goal is of much more worth in the long run than being interrupted by short-term distractions.

The highly disciplined martial artist, movie star and successful businessman Bruce Lee said,

"LONG-TERM CONSISTENCY TRUMPS SHORT-TERM INTENSITY"

MAKING A PLAN IS SIMPLE, following it takes discipline. Start with your daily routine. Depending on how you work best at the moment, either schedule particular times of the day or have set goals that must be completed by the end of the day, without sticking to exact times.

Know when you are most productive.

Do you accomplish more in the morning or in the afternoon?

WHATEVER TIME YOU BEGIN, try to get most of your goals done within the first few hours of starting. This is typically the time when your resilience is at its strongest. As the hours wear on, so too does your ability to wield your willpower to overcome distractions.

KEEP YOUR DAILY GOALS SMART, that is:

1. **Specific:** What do you actually want to achieve? Too specific and you will be disappointed if you don't get that exact relationship, car or job you want, so allow some flexibility.
2. **Measurable:** How long will it take and how will you know when to stop?
3. **Achievable:** Is it small enough to be achievable today or is it too challenging?
4. **Realistic:** Are you being realistic about managing and completing this goal or do you need to lower your expectations?
5. **Time-Bound:** Is the time-frame to complete the action right or does it need adjusting?

Remember that Things Take Time and allow yourself a period of adjustment. Know that some days will be easy and some more difficult. Even on those difficult days, just a small step is building your resilience.

Exercise 14: Stick to your Goals

1. To help yourself achieve your goal, never let more than two days pass without completing your practice or action.
2. Design a chart or calendar where you can tick off the days when you complete your focus task and put a cross when you have not completed the task.
3. If you are about to put your third cross on the calendar, have a good talk with yourself and find a way to complete,

or partially complete it, within the next few hours and then tick your calendar.

4. Know that most people quit too soon because they don't commit to the long-term.

5. Stick to the two-day rule! Never let a third day pass without having practiced or taken a step toward that destination that you are responsible for reaching.

Beware of comfort zones and the complacency they bring

When making new changes, people revert to bad routines and patterns of behaviour that fit in with their old self that they feel comfortable with. Comfort is one of the most difficult addictions in our lives. We are attracted to the status quo, yet at the same time we have an innate nature to improve our conditions. To improve our conditions, we must break the habit of comfort and face elements of risk.

Life will repeat itself until we learn a lesson, and until that time we will keep experiencing it again and again. The only way out is to make the changes that you need.

We adapt too easily to the conditions we get used to, including the negative and the complacent behaviour of not taking action. If you are no longer feeling the slight buzz of happiness that comes from appreciating new experiences through the act of taking small risks, you are likely stuck in a rut. Complacency takes comfort a step further. It comes from being too passive, mentally and physically.

Complacency is letting go of any possible feeling of threat to your well-being. You experience a satisfaction that everything is okay and you don't need to lift a finger or make any effort as everything is quite comfortable as it is. Too much complacency and comfort can be unhealthy for our body and mind as you don't make the effort to care for it.

An exaggerated state of complacency occurs when too much pride leads to a fall. When you are too complacent and ignore dangers and threats, it will lead to you paying the consequences for your deliberate inaction. The ancient Greeks wrote many plays about exaggerated complacency, and called it "hubris." Hubris is the characteristic of excessive confidence or arrogance, which leads a person to believe that he or she may do no wrong.

In Aesop's tale, "The Tortoise and the Hare," about a hare and a tortoise running a race, the hare brags excessively about being faster than the tortoise before the race and then while racing the tortoise. The hare is arrogantly proud and has an inflated ego that they will win against the tortoise. The hare's downfall is the choice to take a nap under a tree during the race, complacently believing that the tortoise will never catch up. Slowly and steadily the tortoise continues until crossing the finish line to win the race. The hare is humiliated at being beaten by the tortoise as a consequence of hubris.

Cartoon character Homer Simpson summed up his fight with complacency over food when he said,

"WHY DO ALL the bad things taste so good?"

Repeating negative actions and self-sabotage

Why do some people repeat same patterns? such as:

- Attract partners who take advantage of them or treat them abusively.
- Gamble or spend away their hard-earned savings or other people's money without their permission.
- Stay stuck in a job they hate.

Most people fear the unknown and take comfort in what they do know. As the old saying goes,

"BETTER THE DEVIL you know than the Devil you don't!"

. . .

WHEN YOU GET comfortable with a negative pattern of behaviour, it begins to become a part of your unconscious identity and becomes an excuse:

"I've always done this."

"It's just a part of who I am."

OR ULTIMATUMS SUCH AS:

"This is how I am. Take it or leave it."

THIS ACCEPTANCE of a negative behaviour is an excuse for change. When it is deeply ingrained, any challenge from another is met with a strong defence.

So why do people cling to these negative beliefs and patterns?

There is an unconscious intention to keep things safe as they are with the hope that things will get better without having to confront their own negative beliefs and behaviours. An individual caught in a negative pattern still feels there is hope that their partner will change or they will win that lottery jackpot or that their pay outweighs the fear of changing jobs and the discomfort of facing something new. Unconsciously the individual is self-sabotaging to keep things at a status quo of what is familiar and comfortable. Taking a risk on something new is too frightening. However, deep down, they do not feel happy about their situation and will often share their discontent with friends and escape into fantasy-life fictions such as books, television and the internet.

WHATEVER WEAKNESS you have will attract more of the same negative experiences until you learn your lesson. Your unconscious mind will keep bringing these experiences to your attention until you consciously take control and make a change. The unconscious mind has your survival and wellbeing in mind; however, it will bring things up in the most indirect of ways. It's 'positive intention' is for you to take action and deal with things differently. When you know this rule, you will be able to make changes without the need for history to keep repeating itself.

Do you keep asking the question,
"Why does this keep happening to me over and over again?"

- You live pay to pay and just don't seem to be able to save money due to so many good spending opportunities or bills.
- Other events happen and you just can't get to the gym as they seem a little more important than becoming healthy.
- You keep making excuses to not go on that date, saying to yourself that the day or time is inconvenient or that you are busy.

Exercise 15: New Actions

1. Look at one of your negative repeating behaviours.
2. Listen to yourself and objectively look at the situation and ask,

- "What am I unconsciously trying to tell myself?"
- "What do I need to do free myself from this pattern and take better, positive actions?"
- "What actions do I need to take?"
- "What action do I need to take right now?"

3. Follow the "Never less than 2 consecutive days" plan to ensure you take action every day and resist the temptation to fall back into old patterns of behaviour.

The importance of risk

"Two roads diverged in a wood, and I, I took the one less travelled by, and that has made all the difference."
Robert Frost

LIFE IS an adventure of travelling and learning. It takes responsibility and effort to tread a new path in the long-term and not take the well-worn short-cuts. If you choose the path less travelled, you will arrive at your destination a very different person to the one who took the shortcut!

You will understand more about how life works and appreciate the capabilities and bravery you drew upon to get to your destination. There will be no need for making excuses and you will be used to choosing how you react to external events. Take the shortcut and you will miss out on opportunities for life-changing experiences.

WHEN ON THE LESS-TRAVELLED PATH, don't be tempted by your own irresponsible excuses or the condescending comments of others to get you back on to the mainstream route:

- "Why do you bother?"
- "Why do you want to be better than everyone else?"
- "What's the point of that?"

Rise above these comments:

- "I will be stronger, more independent and happier
  through my efforts to carve my own way in the world."

Just like the hero's progress in your favourite stories. Trust that you will find a path, after all,
"Where there is a will, there is a way!"

You just need to ensure you have the will and have mapped out a way.

ALONG YOUR PATH, know your goals. Visualise them as if you have already achieved them to get you into the right mindset. You will feel better motivated as the image becomes a part of your unconscious thinking. The more vivid your visualisation and the more you see it through your own eyes, the more compelling it becomes to you. Regularly picturing success, and then putting in the necessary effort and patience needed, will speed up your quest to achieve it. We can only change our life by putting in the commitment and energy necessary into the current moment. That is why when we visualise, we imagine the goal as already achieved. You access all the feelings of your success now, and can perform with greater efficiency as you work toward it. The opposite is when we wish for things for the future, as that is where they stay, as a wish.

Don't Wish, Visualise!

The Pareto Principle or 80/20 rule

The Pareto Principle states that for many outcomes roughly 80% of consequences come from 20% of the causes, known as the "vital few." The Pareto Principle is also known as the 80/20 rule or the "Principle of Factor Sparsity."

Developed by Management Consultant, Joseph Juran, the principle was used to improve quality control, and was named after the Italian Economist, Vilfredo Pareto who researched the pattern of 80/20 in 1896 at the University of Lausanne. In 'Cours d'économie Politique,' Pareto wrote that 80% of the land in Italy was owned by 20% of the population. It is now a common principle used in many aspects of life, from the academic and business fields to the natural world. Although not an exact science, we can take it to mean that a small proportion creates a large proportion.

- A small proportion of clients in a business create most of the profit.
- A small proportion of unhealthy food you eat creates most of the high sugar and fat in your body.
- A small proportion of people in society creates most of the crime.
- A small proportion of the population own most of the money.
- A small proportion of your thinking creates most of your happiness (Imagine 100% of your thinking!)
- A small proportion of your actions create the most results.

WHEN IT COMES to planning your goals and actions, take the most important element contributing to your progress and focus on that as your priority. As you begin to make progress, you can start to focus on the lesser elements of importance. Start with the big picture and work your way to the detail.

In Stephen Covey's book, "The 7 Habits of Highly Effective People" he likens tackling tasks to filling a large mason jar with rocks, gravel, sand and water.

First you fill the jar with the big rocks, then with finer gravel to fill in the gaps, followed with sand to fill the gaps further, and finally with water which fills the jar completely.

You can see the order of thinking. The big rocks fill 80% of the jar with the least input, so you tackle the larger impactful tasks first and then follow up with the final 20% less effective "fillers."

There's no time like the present

Proactive people don't let life just happen to them, they take responsibility and set goals, followed up with actions. Taking charge of what you want leads to feelings of wellbeing and happiness.

Do independent, responsible people care about the response of others to their choices?

Yes, to a point, but not to the extent that they will give up or hinder their happy pursuit for what they enjoy in life. To get started even when others disapprove, know that no time is perfect, so don't wait for the ideal moment. If you really want it, make the time to fit it in and get stuck in to the task. If you are unsure of whether you want it, still give it a go and see if you develop a taste for it. Make sure you enjoy putting in the effort along the way. Every road leads somewhere and no matter where it leads, enjoy the process.

Choosing goals

The strategy for choosing goals is to:

1. Choose a goal compelling enough to excite you.
2. Focus on what strengths you can immediately apply to achieving your goal and not on what you can't.
3. Believe it is a possible goal to achieve and know that if one person can do it, you can learn as well.
4. Ask for advice or help if you need it.
5. Take action at each step and enjoy the journey along the way.

IF A GOAL IS EXCITING, it has to be exciting enough to prevent boredom creeping in. You have to want it. You have to keep thinking about it.

To maintain motivation, ask:

- What will I be capable of when I achieve this new skill or item?
- How will it improve my life?

- How will I happily celebrate achieving each step along the way?
- What is my end point and how will I know I have reached it?
- Does thinking about the challenge make me feel happy with anticipation or fill me with dread?

Keep the following advice in mind:

- Focusing on what you don't want will push your goal away.
- Any "I wish I ......" is a waste of time. Instead, replace an "I wish I ...." with "I am ...., while I ...."

For example:

- Change "I wish I had a different job" to "I am giving my job my best while I seriously look at alternative careers and jobs."
- Change "I wish I had a partner" to "I'm enjoying myself with others when I'm out socially and I'm open to a relationship if I feel a natural attraction."
- Change "I wish I was rich" to "I am making money by putting 20% of my earnings into savings or investments, while I allow my wealth to grow." You can decide the manageable percentage.
- Change "I wish I was more confident" to "I'm growing in confidence as I take one slightly uncomfortable risk each day."

Gaining momentum

You need momentum and momentum comes from the optimistic belief that your efforts and persistence pay off. You embed the seed of your goal into your unconscious mind by thinking about it in an optimistic way as if it is already achieved. Once there it will continue to grow and spread its roots. Eventually, the joy of doing what you visualise in your mind will become automatic as you become more and more comfortable and secure through practice. Only doubt, discomfort or a lack of excitement will prevent that seed from growing.

To get what you want in life, you need to believe it before you see it. Make what you want clear and bright in your mind and the motivation and feelings you need will follow. By believing your goal is a possibility and visualising that you have already attained it, you are already ahead of the many who quit at the first hurdle. You will feel good about it, and secure and comfortable with the idea of attaining it, as in your mind, you already have.

By feeling good when thinking about your goal, you will desire visualising it more often. As a result, you will feel the momentum to take the appropriate actions to reach it. With more momentum and the familiarity of having visualised your achievement a number of times, you will have more confidence dealing with the obstacles you face.

Alongside this confidence, your persistence will provide you with the progress you need to work toward your goal. Persistent people are motivated to work hard to achieve; whereas the naturally talented rarely have the same work ethic or burning passion. Just because you are naturally talented in a particular area does not mean that you enjoy it. If you are, then you have the advantage of already being on a rewarding path.

Exercise 16: Current Position and Future Ambition

Create a "Current Position and Future Ambition" poster.

This can be done digitally or manually. I have outlined the manual process.

1. Take an A3 sized sheet of card for your background.
2. Leave space for a title to be written later.
3. Find images that capture the things in life that you feel

happy about now and inspiring images for the things in life that you would like to improve.

4. Paste on all the images mixing the present and future images together, so that you feel motivated when looking at it. By mixing the images it will help you visualise the future as occurring now.

5. In the gaps between the images, write down the positive feelings you associate with the images. The feelings do not need to be organised in any order, just so that you are able to clearly read them.

6. Decide the positive title you would like for your poster:

7. "I already have all of this now"

8. "This is My Life"

9. Pin it in your workspace or at the end of your bed where you can consciously (and unconsciously) see it.

10. It is important to focus on what you want and not on what you don't want. Remember, like attracts like.

11. Use these feelings as a reminder right this moment that you can experience them now to help compel you toward achieving your goal.

Create a sense of urgency by setting deadlines

Once you know your desired outcome, move backwards each preceding step. Write down the action required to achieve each step until you reach your very first action. Set a date for the completion of each action. Using SMART goals, set realistic dates for the completion of each action.

On top of each action, set daily, repeatable practices to meet.

For example, if you are learning a particular piece on the piano, set a date for when you can play it fluently with expression. Step backwards and set the parts you are going to master at each date until you get to the very first action. Your daily practice of choice may be practicing the particular scale that matches the piece, 20 times in the

morning and 20 times in the evening. Putting a number on your practice makes it practical.

If running 10 km is your goal, plan the distance you wish to run,
and by what date you wish to run it. Step backwards and plan each
goal achievement which may be descending distances by certain
dates until you get to the first. Your daily practice may be to warm up
and stretch for ten minutes to improve your performance.

For experiencing more happiness as your goal, plan to be happy
in a situation you feel uncomfortable in by a certain date, such as an
upcoming party, meeting or family dinner. Plan backwards with
actions to take, leading up to the event. With a plan to be consciously
happy in specific situations and with deadlines, you will have a map
for action. Your practice each day may be an affirmation like, "Today I
will look for the good in every situation" or "I will smile and say "Hi"
to one person I pass by when I am out.""

HERE IS a structure you might use to plan your goal and the actions
you might take.

My goal: Give only positive and constructive suggestions in the
monthly Board Meeting.

Daily Practice: I will reframe 3 negative thoughts to positives every
evening before going to sleep.

- 7th step just before goal: Stand tall, put a smile on my face
  and take a deep breath before entering the boardroom.
- 6th step: Be positive for a full working day in the face of any
  challenge that comes up.
- 5th step: Stand tall and intentionally smile at every person I
  speak with today.
- 4th step: In the evening, reflect on how many challenges
  came up today at work and how I could have handled
  them in a happy and positive way.
- 3rd step: Visualise how people in the Board Meeting will
  notice my happiness, ease and confidence.

- 2nd step: Say "Thank you" with a smile to the barista at the coffee shop today.
- Very 1st action: Smile and say "Hi" to one person while I am out today.

Exercise 17: Preparing for the Best

1. Choose an event with a deadline and how you wish to feel and behave at that event.
2. Write down the very last action you need to take in preparation just before the event takes place.
3. Write down each preceding action you will practice on the way to that event and give each a deadline.
4. Write down the very first action you will take.
5. Decide what simple daily, repetitive practice you can take that best contributes to achieving your goal. Give it a number of repetitions that is manageable and improves your desired goal.

How we build our happiness

When you feel happy, you are more open to opportunities and see the good in people. The more you practice optimism, the more positive your foundation for coping with life events.

In any new learning you undertake, it is important to build your walls and roof upon strong footings and a solid foundation.

- The footings are dug into the ground to support the foundation. Your footings for happiness is knowing in your core that positive thinking trumps negative thinking every single time. Positive actions for the good of yourself and others is the best choice.
- The foundation is built upon the footings and consists of your daily practice, and your routine response to dealing

with negative thoughts. It means being consciously grateful for what you already have and reframing your negative thinking to positive thoughts that you can take action on.

- The walls are formed from the actions you take towards your goal, brick-by-brick. You might hold yourself up and smile before entering any new space, you might decide to smile and say "Hi" to one person each day on your way to work.
- The windows allow you to open up to new experiences and outside teachers and role-models, including podcasts or YouTube instructors.
- The roof caps all the hard work you have done to seal your building from the negative elements; in other words, you've attained the knowledge and experience to better deflect any new setbacks as they arise. You may decide that you are more capable of being happy in any circumstance as your outlook drift to the silver lining of any ominous dark cloud. Your actions are directed toward what you can control.

Adaptability and flexibility

A flexible approach to your goal is important. Circumstances change at the drop of a hat and you need the ability to adapt without stress bringing you to a halt. Focusing on the positive alleviates stress, and taking action on what you have control over, is the method for any change of course or pitfall.

I mentioned in the SMART goal description that you will be disappointed if you are too specific in what you want. Maybe that exact person you desire may not wish to be in a relationship with you or they may not in reality meet your high expectations for what you thought they were. That great, new job in your dream company may not be all that it's cracked up to be. Realise that there are other exciting paths to follow, you just need to be more flexible in your expectations of others, your desired roles or gaining certain material possessions. Things will likely never be exactly as you want as you cannot control the world outside of your own thoughts, attitudes and reactions.

Choosing material goods as goals will also not please you for long. Having previously discussed the 'hedonic treadmill,' your initial high of possessing something new quickly returns to a normal state of satisfaction and happiness. Continue on this path of finding happiness in things, and before you know it, you will be pursuing that next great shiny thing to get those feelings back. It is not sustainable.

Goalposts are always changing, and we are always striving to achieve that very next desire. It is part of our human nature for survival to better our situation and pass on the best we can to our offspring. Happiness is a state of being, a choice, it is not dependent on your goals; however, goals give us the momentum to learn something new and better our lives and the lives of our family.

IT MAY BE A PARADOX, but along with your pursuit of goals, is your need to let go. It is all about achieving contentment and learning to not care so much when things don't work out as you expect they will.

7

IT IS AS IT IS, FORGIVE AND MOVE ON
NO WORRIES, JUST ACCEPTANCE

Life can be an emotional rollercoaster and our emotions affect us both positively and negatively, physically and mentally. An emotion is a signal that we have been stirred in reaction to an event. Our feelings have been triggered and the flood of emotions that follow are our mostly unconscious expression of them in the quickest way possible.

Have you noticed that the more emotional you get about things, the less control you have over them, and people take notice? An accepting person will empathise and help put you at ease. They are in touch with their emotions. Other people will see emotions as a sign of weakness and vulnerability and some of them will try to use this to their advantage. This makes you feel even worse after the situation. To keep a measure of control over your emotions takes a deep acceptance that this control lies within yourself. You have to pick up on every strong emotion that arises and say,

"Stop for a moment. What issue is this emotion trying to bring to my attention?"

Only then can you choose to respond with positive actions and replies in even the most challenging circumstances. This means buying some time to cool off if you are feeling a strong emotion in reaction to another person and they are in your present company. You can:

- Take a deep breath, hold and release.
- Excuse yourself for a moment.
- Gently but literally bite your tongue.
- Ask to put the conversation to the side until later.
- Ask for a moment to think.

If someone is insistent that it needs to be dealt with right there and then you can assert yourself and say one or a mix of the following,

- "I have every right to discuss this when I feel ready. I need time to get my thoughts together."
- "I feel I am being pressured into giving an answer for something I am not ready to respond to at the moment. I will come back to you as soon as I have considered my response."
- "You have obviously had time to compose what you are saying, I would also like to have time to respond."

Triggers of negative emotions

The quickest way to lose control of your negative emotions is to:

- Interpret an event as unjust or cruel, such as natural disasters and human conflicts.
- Argue against another's beliefs or opinions, whether they be political, cultural, religious and equality issues.
- Rise up to the verbal or physical challenge of another in order to preserve your alpha status, such as a threat that belittles you, particularly in public.
- Overly interpreting someone's interest as more than they

intend, such as assuming a friendship or a romantic
interest.

- Attempt to beat a deliberately unbalanced system where
  the odds are in its favour, such as gambling and
  criminality.

Negative emotions without taking positive responsibility for
them, leads to criticism and complaining. Criticising events outside
of your control will raise your sensitivity to the many injustices of the
world. Dwelling on the negative feelings they evoke will either stir
you to take positive action or simply lead you to becoming another
negative complainer in society.

When you practice entertaining too many negative thoughts, you
begin responding with mainly negative emotions and actions. This
opens up a Pandora's Box of further problems. If you respond angrily
to a provocative comment or action , you instantly become a threat
and will likely receive anger in return. Afterwards, you will likely feel
regret or even more anger. This may well have been the intention of
the other party to provoke your negative response publicly.

Things work out differently when you respond with understanding, warmth, caring, empathy and active listening. Any good intention to improve a misunderstanding, usually defuses a difficult
situation. If you respond in a congenial and positive way, the other
party won't view you as a threat or challenge to them.

Empathy

If you feel empathy for others, you are accepting the right that others
have their own opinions and beliefs, just as you have your own. You
may disagree with them entirely; however, you know that their reactions have been shaped by their beliefs and you can separate their
behaviour from who they are as a human. Forgiveness is the practice
of acceptance, and when we accept and forgive ourselves first, we stop
the criticism and are more open to forgiving others.

.   .   .

ELVIS PRESLEY SANG the following words in "Walk A Mile in my Shoes,"

"BEFORE YOU ABUSE, criticise and accuse, walk a mile in my shoes."

ACCEPTANCE IS LETTING GO of assuming the meaning of outside events; the old saying goes,
"When I assume, I make an ass out of you and me!"
Making assumptions mostly leads to viewing an event in a negative way. When you have made an assumption, ask:

* "What exactly is the evidence that backs up my assumption?"

Acceptance and forgiveness does not mean rolling on your back with your legs in the air and allowing a storm of arguments, opinions or physical harm happen batter you into submission. Oppressive beliefs, behaviours and injustice are very real in our world. Instead of resorting to conflict, which we know increases defensiveness and offensiveness, our first path is to choose to influence or inspire a change through the positive role-modelling of better alternatives. We have total power in controlling how we react to events, and we have some power to inspire change toward what is happening in our world. Most of all we have a code of human rights to live by, outlined earlier in the book.

The most effective way to inspire change in others is by being a role-model for the change you want to see happening. If you lead by example, those who share similar beliefs will follow or you can follow them. The only other choice for you to make a change in the world is control, through manipulation, threat and confrontation. However, manipulation, threat and confrontation provoke an immediate defensive position from other parties. You must expect that those opposed to your control will fight you directly or find ways to fight you behind your back, using their own manipulation.

Most illustrations of conflict describe a battle; you must win the most battles in order to win the war: The battle of the sexes, the war on crime/drugs etc. In modern times it is more civilised to positively inspire change and win people's hearts and minds. To inspire change in others is to offer benefits that will improve their lives or protect them from their perceived fears.

People tend to be inspired by those who encourage their dreams or calm their fears. This is how having a happy and optimistic approach to life attract friendships. Unfortunately, people are also influenced by others who fuel their suspicions and join their side against their perceived enemies. This is where a cynical and negative approach to life can create a following of those who distrust other people; however, conspiracy theories and blame will not lead to feelings of happiness.

Accepting and forgiving life and its imperfection

By accepting life and its imperfections now, you end the perception that life is unjust. You don't waste time pondering life as an endless struggle of painful events and suffering. Instead, you constructively manage what is in your path right now. Let go and appreciate, look for the good and enjoy the moment.

Your happiness and success depend on the knowledge that like attracts like. To attract good things, knowing that peace starts with you, is the best place to begin, by being grateful for what you have right now. By counting your blessings, gratitude will give you greater power than counting your misfortunes.

When you are grateful for your friends, family, and what you already have in your life, you are more likely to connect with better people, experiences and opportunities.

If you criticise, condemn or complain, you receive more of the same.

Difficult people in your life may project their own pain upon you. Whether they do it consciously or unconsciously, remember, you are ultimately in control of your reactions. As difficult as it can be, you must learn to forgive them. If you don't forgive them, that resentment eats you up from the inside and poisons your thoughts and feelings.

Forgiving does not mean giving in to wrongdoing, you must still assert your rights if someone is causing you abusive harm. If their behaviour toward you is illegal, you can seek help from the law or from your union for workplace-related matters.

Typically, people will respond with upset, anger and even revenge to being fired by their boss or dumped by their partner and we can all objectively recognise this is the wrong response. If you decide you will never forgive your boss or ex-partner, their lives will simply move forward, and you will continue yours with pain and suffering as you continue to ask, "Why me?"

Unfortunately, the answer to that question is "Why not!" It can happen to anyone.

The best approach is to forgive them knowing it was not meant to be and there are better times ahead; be patient and persistent, Things Take Time and you need to focus on what you can do in the moment, not what you can't control.

Anger, resentment and other negative feelings will cause your mental and physical health to decline. By internally giving in by ruminating on harmful feelings, you will now project them to everyone else in your life.

If you seek any form of revenge, this reflects your dependence on others for your own self-worth. Independent people move on and focus on their own progress in life.

Forgiveness is strength

I reiterate that forgiveness is not giving in. You do not have to agree with what someone did to you, you let go and accept that it has happened. It is now in the past. You want to learn from what has happened, seek legal representation if required, and then move your life back and focus on all the positive possibilities that come with a happy and optimistic view. The longer you hold onto the past, the longer it will take for new opportunities to present themselves to you.

Stop the fight, stop the worry and start to let go. Let the good into your life and let go of the bad. As they say, "In with the good, out with the bad." Keep hold of the 20% of people, experiences and possessions that bring happiness and serves a positive purpose and let go of the 80% that simply don't make the grade.

Exercise 18: Your Own Personal Protective Barrier

1. Imagine a ring drawn around your feet or a column of energy surrounding you, about a metre in circumference. This represents a barrier between what is within your circle of direct control and what is outside of your circle of control.
2. Know that this barrier is within your personal control only. It follows you everywhere and it protects you from the effects of outside events. You can accept what you want within it and reject what you don't want.
3. Search for negative elements inside the barrier that you no longer wish to have. Maybe they are certain thoughts that make you feel weak. Maybe they are behaviours that make you feel bad. Maybe they are negative comments that others have said to you.
4. Turn them into representations, such as a photo, a written note or a recording.
5. Recognise the unconscious positive intention they might

have meant to serve and then forgive them for the unintentional pain they may have caused, e.g. "I know you were trying to help me avoid future situations where I might feel upset and I forgive you for the actual pain you caused me."

6. Since you no longer want them within your circle of control, open your barrier, push them outside, and then close your barrier. You can imagine putting them into a bin, a shredder, fire or incinerator. You can imagine scattering them outside as petals and the wind carrying them through the air.

7. Now imagine some aspects of the outside world that you would like to bring into yourself. Maybe you want to feel more positivity and happiness. Turn your idea of strength into a positive representation, e.g. a warm glowing ball of light, whatever best represents this feeling to you.

8. Open your barrier and draw this representation toward you. Once it is inside, close your barrier and bring it inside of your body. Let it settle in the area you feel is the centre of your happiness, such as your chest.

9. Thank this feeling for now being a new and positive part of you.

Facing a fear

Letting go of fear is one of the most difficult challenges we all have. Fears are mostly imagined as they haven't yet happened. When we are presented with a new challenge, we tend to unconsciously ascend the following steps:

STEP 8. I did it!
    Step 7. I will do it
    Step 6. I can do it
    Step 5. I'll give it a go

Step 4. How do I do it?

Step 3. I want to do it?

Step 2. I can't do it!

Step 1. I won't do it

ACCEPTING that you will have to face challenges on any journey, and knowing that there is a positive end if you make the effort, will help allay your fears. This is the same process for feeling happy and positive. For any pain, relief will come. You can always find something a little positive even in the most tragic of circumstances.

You may feel that life isn't fair, or you may feel that life is fair. With a view of acceptance, life just is what it is.

When you need to let things pass, think,

"IT IS WHAT IT IS!"

THE UNIVERSE DOESN'T ACKNOWLEDGE what you think or feel, the Universe just is. Only you or your closest family and friends may care about your wellbeing, and you can do yourself and your loved ones a favour by accepting responsibility for your positive reactions to life. If you feel good, they will feel good for you.

What is life?

Life is what you make it. It doesn't happen to you; you express what life is through the reality that you choose. By choosing a reality of acceptance, you can be happy and content that you don't have to worry about the big things out of your control. Look for beauty in the simple things. Reframe the ugliness that provokes your negative reaction by focusing on the silver linings. If you feel compelled to improve the ugliness in the world, you can inspire change as a role-model for that change you wish to see.

It's not what happens to you that is important, it is how you feel about what happens to you. Much of what happens is just not worth your reaction. Let go and learn from any of the negative reactions you have made. Focus on how you can react differently and positively now.

When you fight what is out of your control, you lose every single time. Accept it and say,

"THERE'S nothing I can do about it except change my reaction to it or inspire a change."

WHEN DORIS DAY sang the lyrics in the song "Que Sera, Sera," she profoundly summarised what acceptance is. "Que Sera, Sera" translates from Spanish to, "What will be, will be."

"QUE SERA, Sera
  Whatever will be, will be
  The future's not ours to see
  Que Sera, Sera
  What will be, will be."

EVERY CHALLENGE or tragedy in your life can go in either two directions, sinking into negativity and despair, or accepting it for what it is and identifying the positive learning that will be helpful to yourself and possibly others.

Detachment

Buddhism teaches a form of acceptance through detachment from worldly things, such as other people or possessions. Buddhists believe that attachment to people and things will ultimately lead to suffering. There is only impermanence in our physical world and you cannot keep a hold on anything material.

When we chase what we desire, it often seems to retreat from our grasp. It's as if our desperation scares away our desire. When we let go of the chase, we start to attract the very things we were chasing.

One of the most powerful affirmations to say to yourself each and every day to relieve any feeling of desperation is,

- **"I already have all that I need."**

WITH THIS STATEMENT, the desperation stops, and we start to notice the opportunities around us.

Detachment does not mean being disinterested and disassociated from the world. Being detached means you can still be driven to achieve your goals. You simply accept and let go of events beyond your control that would normally thwart you and raise your negative reactions. Effort and persistence continue to be required but you let go of your expectations for certain results. It is not the result that determines your happiness. You have chosen to live a life of being mostly happy, regardless of outcomes; e.g. you go for that job, you give that audition a shot, or you attempt that world record. You do so in a relaxed state of acceptance, letting go any expectation you will get the position, win that role or break that record. Instead, you focus on giving your best in the moment.

Afterward, you get on with the rest of your life without desperation tugging at your thoughts and causing anxiety. Your actions were enough for you to be proud, and any other positive result is a bonus.

You are most likely to achieve in a relaxed state than in a desperate and anxious state. A little bit of anxiety provides some motivation, but a lot is a problem.

Giving without expectation

A part of accepting and letting go, is giving. You give with the intention to help another with something they can't do themselves, without expecting anything in return. If you give in the expectation of a return, it is no longer giving, it is now a transaction; you should either not give in the first place or just state what you want in return for your gift. Only give if you can do so free of expectations of a return. Giving is unconditional.

Giving unconditionally can open a network of positive events. The 2000 movie "Pay It Forward" is a great example of creating a network of giving. In the movie, rather than giving a gift in return, the 11-year-old lead main character creates a plan for paying a good deed forward to another person. The recipient then pays forward three favours to three different people who could not have achieved the favour by themselves. This practice of multiplying good deeds spreads virally across the country spreading happiness.

As adults we teach children that "Sharing is caring," yet so many of us can't do the same without expectations of a return. We confuse giving with conducting business. When we give to others out of a feeling of duty, guilt or social expectations, we aren't giving willingly. We don't truly feel the emotions that come from giving our love or caring. Anonymous giving is the ultimate giving. There are no expectations, indeed possibility of a return, apart from knowing that we may have made a difference to someone else's life. The positive energy you express may well pay forward to others by those who have received your generosity of giving.

Inhibitions and resistance

Children exude an energy and naivety that is boundless in its purity. Everything is new and exciting. They have their ideas and they put them into action making use of the limited resources they have and filling the gaps with their borderless imaginations.

What will block or limit their imaginations is interference by adults. Adults tend to impose teaching that follows rules and structures and limit the child's "What if" thoughts with adult thoughts of "What must happen in order to...." As mature adults, our once childlike acceptance that we can imagine or do anything has been quashed by taking on a fixed role, earning a living, paying bills, and manoeuvring the world without offending anyone. Our energy gets blocked. So too does our happiness and ability to notice all the positive opportunities for change that surround us.

Signs of blocking positive energy and opportunities presents in many forms. You are chatting with someone but it doesn't flow because they don't use open replies and the conversation comes to a halt. You wish to start a business and are excited by the idea but the only responses you get from your nearest and dearest are,

"90% of businesses fail in their first 12 months!"

"Good luck with that then."

"That's a bit of a risk isn't it?"

Resistance is blocking the flow of energy and we encounter it all the time.

THE AMERICAN FABLE of the "Little Red Hen?" is a prime tale of making an effort but feeling resistance from others at every step.

The Little Red Hen decides to bake bread and she asks each of her friends to help with the various stages of preparing the ingredients and baking it. When she cuts, gathers and threshes the grain from the wheat, the dog, the cat and the little duck won't help and make their excuses. When she mills the flour and bakes the bread, the dog, the cat and the little duck won't help and make their excuses. However, when she asks them, "Who will help me eat the bread?" they all spring up and offer to eat it. Does she say "No" to them? She shares the bread.

WITH WISDOM, the Little Red Hen has applied acceptance and giving. She has learned to accept that creating something takes an idea and hard work, that others will resist that idea and hard work, and that when someone creates their own success, suddenly everyone takes an interest. Having her high standards to create the bread but low expectations of support from others, the Little Red Hen gets on with the job, completes it and shares her success without misgivings. She does not allow her energy to be blocked.

YOU BLOCK your own energy by making excuses and foreseeing all the pitfalls ahead of you. You state, "What if this happens?" before you have even started, and it immediately halts your progress.

To defeat this negative thinking, know that you already have all the personal inner strengths and resources you need to get started. You also have the potential to learn new strategies along the way to get around any obstacles, if you persist. Imagine that you have already achieved the goal and feel those feelings of success now. Accept what you already have to give and know that any achievement requires work, effort, patience and resilience. We are all capable of building resilience and therefore we are all capable of pursuing what we feel excited or motivated by.

Acceptance is the opposite of giving up. Acceptance is knowing that a journey can be completed the hard way through lots of personal resistance or an easier path where you expect obstacles, and you accept that you have the inner resources and the ability to learn new things to manage them. Acceptance is moving forwards; resistance is staying stuck. Acceptance is seeing things objectively, "It is what it is." Things are okay and there is always another way to improve a situation; there are always alternatives.

When we operate from a feeling of happiness, we accept that:

- Challenges can be resolved.
- That arguing is pointless.
- That resistance is just blocking progress when you should be exploring solutions instead.
- That criticising, complaining and condemning is the

irresponsible behaviour of blaming external things outside of our personal control.

Operating from happiness is always looking for the positive, the good, the silver lining in the most challenging of situations. It is the most powerful personal trait you can exercise. It is also the fastest path to maintaining feelings of happiness as you are no longer consumed by others' opinions and expectations.

TO LEAD A HAPPY LIFE, you don't need to know the outcome of every-thing, or understand everything, or work toward being the best of the best. Acceptance is appreciating the positives around you and allowing that energy to continue flowing throughout your life.

ACCEPTING that you can improve will change your life if you:

- Still think people are the cause of your problems.
- Think your environment is the cause of your problems.
- Feel you are stuck.
- Resist moving forward in any area of your life.
- Wait for things to happen to improve your life.
- Don't think you can ever be happy, successful, positive or improve in any way.
- Your beliefs are persistently negative.
- You wish for more thinking it will solve your problems.
- You think someone else will change your life for you.

Meditation and letting go

Relax your habit of critical thinking and you will notice more opportu-nities around you. By meditating, you can help release and relax doubts, concerns and issues that persist in occupying your moment-to-moment thinking. Meditation can be as simple as allowing thoughts to pass through your mind without judgement. When you transfix your attention in the moment, you are entering a meditative state; looking at a candle flame, watching your children play, observing nature such as a bird or a tree swaying in the breeze or a stream flowing. You can even watch fixed nature scenes on YouTube, designed to put you at ease. Any exercise or activity that absorbs your attention fully can be considered a moving meditation as long as your thoughts are focused in those present movements and not in the past or the future.

Exercise 19: A Quick Moment for Meditation

1. Find a space to relax and focus. It can be quiet or noisy, depending on your ability to focus your attention inward. Quiet is best for beginners.
2. You can sit or lay down. Sitting comfortable may well prevent you from falling asleep.
3. You can close your eyes or you can stare at a fixed object. Closing your eyes will block out visual distraction and focus inward. Staring at an object may bring you into a glazed over, trance-like state.
4. When you are in a relaxed state, start to notice the thoughts passing through your mind. Allow them to drift past without any interference or analysis.
5. Notice whether they are thoughts from the past, present or future.
6. To help let these thoughts go, label them. Simply say in your mind, "I accept you from a past that is no longer " or "I accept you as a future thought that hasn't happened," or simply label them "past" or "future."
7. Your objective is to have moments of no thoughts, by allowing what is on your mind to pass you by, you are

starting a process of emptying your thoughts and being in the present moment.

8. Let go of expectations of how long you should have no thoughts for. You may well have a mind full of thoughts in one session, seconds of no thoughts in another session, or minutes in another. This happens to even seasoned meditators.

9. There is no magic or mystique to this method of meditating. There are many types of meditation you can explore if you wish to follow a spiritual approach.

IN YOUR SEARCH TO find the answers to life, whether you travel the world, read vast numbers of books or study with great teachers, know that you can also find many answers within. Let go and accept the things that are out of your control and focus on the way you react to your world through acceptance, forgiveness, unconditional giving and knowing that you inspire others by the way you personally live your life.

8

RELATING HAPPILY WITH OTHERS
WORDS AND ACTIONS COUNT MORE WHEN OTHERS ARE CONSIDERED

R elationships can be the most complex area of our lives. We naturally get emotionally attached to the people in our lives through our social interactions and reliance upon one another. Other people enhance our life and for many, other people validate their life. We are social beings out of our necessity to survive. Where we fall short in our relationships is having to second guess the thoughts of others. As we cannot read minds, this can lead to many misunderstandings and frustration over differing expectations and responses.

If you are too attached to someone else's approval, you have developed a dependency on them. Emotional attachment is a neediness and reliance on another to make yourself feel valued, accepted and of worth. This we know is not sustainable. We need to be independent and have control over our own emotional states and reactions if we are to lead a happy and positive life.

Relationships are a delicate balance of push and pull. When we appear desperate and are chasing someone for their attention, we tend to push them away by our over-eagerness.

Sometimes people want more from us than we want from them and vice-versa. As long as you know that you are not reliant on another for your emotional state of being, your expectations for a fair give-and-take in the relationship will be more balanced.

The most important aspect of being in any relationship and friendship is to remain true to yourself, positive and happy. People don't want to be around a ball of misery unless it supports their own feelings of misery. This is what you find in a co-dependent relationship where the parties support one another's negative traits and habits. The danger lies in them reinforcing dependency in a vicious cycle.

Giving to those close to you

Being positive does not mean giving advice all the time and parenting your friend. People typically don't want advice unless they ask for it. You are not there to change your friend, it is their responsibility to decide if they want to change, perhaps with the support of a coach or therapist. You only need to show your approval for their desire for a positive change.

When you are happy, positive support of another person means seeing the bright side of every situation even when they are pulling the conversation into a dark place. The best thing you can do is listen and empathise. If they ask for your advice, reply with your beliefs or the actions you take that work for your own wellbeing. Don't present them with conjecture about what might work for them which you haven't experienced for yourself. It may backfire if they take your advice and it doesn't work for them.

Congruence, integrity and identity

When we don't behave like our true selves, we are not operating from our own area of control but trying to please someone outside of us. In other words, we are trying to impress others by proving that we are popular, intellectual, tough, cool, attractive, wealthy or poor. When you don't act from your authentic self, you come across as incongruous and people will see through you.

You are more likely to impress someone else by being yourself, being natural and not appearing desperate. When someone is behaving from desperation with you, it seems unnatural, you feel like they are trying to trap or control you in some way. You feel that they are so dependent on you that they will not let you alone. You do not want to lose your independence and personal opportunities at the expense of someone else. When you are independent in your actions and thinking, people respect you for knowing what you want, where you want to go, and having integrity.

People can quickly fall into dependency when they lose their sense of identity. They quickly lose control over their reactions and emotions and can't seem to find anything that inspires them. They tend to influence the world through bribery, selfish demands, and emotional manipulation, giving all their control to the outside world and completely weakening their self-integrity and reputation with others. The more you help them, the more dependent they become as they lose all effort to be bothered. When others are serving them and making them feel comfortable, why should you bother making an effort?

How we help others who are dependent upon us is by not helping them much at all. We bring their attention to their strengths and then encourage them to draw upon them, but we don't do everything for them. When someone is knocked down by a life event, they need to learn to stand back up on their own two feet with your patience and positive encouragement of their strengths. Remember, you are not their coach or therapist and there to offer advice, you are their family or friend. When they feel independent again, they will feel happy through their own sense of self-sufficiency.

Dependency gives rise to sacrifice

Do you sacrifice your own needs for other's?

Treat yourself as your own best friend first until you feel your self-integrity is strong enough to assertively manage the demands of others. If you are full of self-criticism, know that you would not treat your best friend the way that you are treating yourself. When you are self-integrated and feeling positive and happy, you are in a much better position to give support unconditionally. If you are caught out by the urgent needs of a friend, just listen, but make no promises of help unless you are sure you can manage it. By listening only, your friend will hopefully come to conclusions of how to help themselves, having talked out the situation.

Compliments, not flattery

Most people feel that what they do goes unrecognised. This applies to children and adults of all ages. A compliment is the most simple and effective unconditional gift you can give to anyone, when it is done correctly. You are expressing positive love and like to a person when you compliment them, and most of us are pleasantly surprised when we receive it. Most people will react with feelings of, "You have made my day!" when receiving a sincere and heart-felt compliment from the appreciation it communicates. A compliment is different to flattery. Flattery is usually delivered with an ulterior motive for personal gain. An excessive and exaggerated comment with no specific reference to the admired characteristic or action. Notice how shallow over-generalised flattery sounds:

- "You are always so wonderful at everything you do"
- "Is there anything you are not perfect at?"
- "You are such a hard worker"
- "You're the best boss"

COMPLIMENTARY PRAISE SHOULD ALWAYS BE personable and specific:

- "The colour of your top really matches your positive energy today."

- "I really appreciate your kindness. You always make time to listen to me."
- "I learn so much when you talk about your cooking. It really inspires me to cook more when I get home."
- "Every time I find myself in a spot of trouble, you notice and help. Thank you."
- "You've paid so much attention to the detail of your story, and it especially shows in the description of your setting."
- "I love being around your positive energy, it rubs off on me, and makes my day."

WHENEVER YOU RECEIVE A COMPLIMENT, accept it and say, "Thank you." If you respond with all the reasons why you are not worthy of this compliment, you will block the flow of positive energy. By giving and receiving compliments, happiness flows.

Confrontation leads to confrontation

In the previous chapter we looked at why confrontation leads to defensiveness and anger. It happens between countries and it happens between people. Trying to change people is a no-no. Keep in mind that if you do try to actively change someone and it doesn't work out and meet their expectations or your promises, they will likely resent you or even hate you for your interference. People will ask if they need help or you can ask them if they would like yours, but only in the support of them personally choosing to take responsibility for their own change.

Many people enter relationships thinking that they can change that little bit of their partner that is a problem. There should be no therapy or coaching in a relationship, especially a romantic relationship, just a listening ear and encouragement. Changing addictions and strongly formed behaviours such as drinking, gambling and smoking are very difficult, changing beliefs near impossible. You should enter the relationship with no thoughts that your partner needs to change. That change has to be in their control or the hands of a professional. Outside help from a professional is always the best support for people with addictions or habitual, inappropriate behaviour. You just can't 'fix' people like you can fix objects, they have to undergo a process of change themselves, willingly:

They have to understand the consequences of their actions and learn personal responsibility, not blame outside sources.

These consequences may lead them to the depths of desperation before they make the decision to change.

They need to take action to escape the pain and move toward the pleasure of achieving the new behaviour they desire.

Ironically they will likely face even more pain as they step out from their habituated comfort zone.

They will need to draw upon their own resilience and strength to see them through the eleventh hour of change.

Close relationships

Your happiness in relationships comes from your ability to accept your minor flaws and the minor flaws of other people. If their flaws are deeper and cause you or others harm, then they should be encouraged to seek appropriate help if they want the relationship to continue. If you have good self-worth and are assertive and independent enough, you know not to put up with any deliberate harm. If they are very difficult or a danger to themselves or others, then seek the appropriate professional help you need to protect them and yourself from harm.

No one else can make us happy, they can only enhance the happiness we already feel inside. There are plenty of miserable people out there whose partners are optimistic, happy and positive. In a functioning relationship, you will share your own happiness and your positive outlook on life, and you will both appreciate it.

To UNDERSTAND one another in a relationship we need to realise that every person values things differently. Some of us value practical things and some of us value personal things, and some of us value a mix of both.

- Practical things solve problems and are in the form of logical advice, physical tools or a sequence of actions that get results.
- Personal things involve the emotion and intention behind them, the aesthetics of their appearance, compliments, and appreciation.

When you are giving a gift or a compliment, keep in mind that if you give something practical to a person who prefers something personal, they may receive it with some disappointment.

The danger of interfering in relationships

Be very careful when interfering with others' relationships. There could be unforeseen consequences. If you have ever had a close friend or family member who has been in a consistent on and off relationship, giving advice is treading into the danger zone. Imagine a close friend comes to you heartbroken, with tales of mistreatment, neglect and woe. Being the good friend, you advise them on all the reasons that they are not suited to be together and perhaps they are best separating. The next day you see that they are back together, walking down the street holding hands. Only yesterday you previously expressed your belief to your friend that they are not really suited together. You later find out your friend has shared all of what you said with their partner. Believe me, this happens a lot!

Advising others in their relationships should be considered a dangerous topic just as being a therapist or a coach in your own relationship can lead to resentment.

Expressing love

If you knew that you only had a short time left to live and you would no longer be able to tell your significant others how much you love them and care for them, do you think that would make a difference with how you relate to them now?

There is no need to wait for a tragic event to express your love or appreciation. The only guaranteed time you have is now, and it mustn't slip away with you being stubborn or cautious about your affections.

IF YOU ARE LOOKING to express your love, you need to feel like you are loved and loveable yourself. A family member or close friend should be able to affirm your feeling that you are loved or at least liked very much.

For those who are looking for a partner to love, trusting that you are capable of loving another is important for your morale. There is someone for everyone, probably many; as they used to say in the past, "There is a lid for every pot."

By being yourself and not out to impress, you are likely to connect with someone more suitable to you than if you were to put on an act and attract the wrong person. Enhance your honesty with a smile, a happy attitude and a positive outlook, and your chances of attracting the right person are even stronger. Don't wait for that person to come along to make you happy. Be happy now and you will notice the positive people who come your way. Play out your strengths and you will attract people with similar mindsets and create positive opportunities to connect. People are generally not attracted to negativity and misery unless they wish to "fix" you or have you in their company to reinforce their own negativity and misery.

Your number one relationship is with yourself, not your family, partner, friends or work colleagues. Your happiness comes from you and not from them. Others can enhance or influence your happiness and you can enhance and inspire their happiness by projecting positive thoughts and actions outwards.

If you continue to struggle with your relationship with yourself, you deserve to know you are worthy of everything you believe others are worthy of. Rather than treating others better than yourself, treat yourself better first and you will have more to give to others. Do not judge yourself in an unfair way.

If you believe there is a God out there who gives unconditional love to all souls equally, why can't you give unconditional love to yourself. If you believe in the mathematical laws of the Universe, why can't you see that you live under the same equal laws as everyone else.

Be kind to yourself. Your happiness benefits the world around you, and is not an act of selfishness. Every experience you will ever have is shaped by the feelings you had for yourself in that moment. Your whole history is coloured by your past thoughts and feelings. If you want to have consistently good memories, you have to love yourself in the current moment, not wait for it to happen at some future external event for which you have no guarantee.

Loving yourself is simply respecting that you are a worthy person. You live with the acceptance that when seemingly bad things happen, "It is what it is." You can get on and react to events in a positive way and improve on what you have learned from them. Growth comes from our challenges and how we face them; stagnation comes from retreating and avoiding those very same challenges through the fear of something that has not yet happened.

Self-determination

People who accept themselves and give their love are optimistic and generate a positive energy which others feel. Their functional relationship with themselves means that they simply can't take things personally. The quickest way to desperately struggle with life is to take a negative view and allow all the possibilities to pass you by as you are too fearful to take a risk; the outside world is controlling you.

Instead, you must control your personal attitudes and reactions to the events in the outside world.

ONE OF THE most profound and simple statements on self-determination and acceptance is from the Buddhist monk Thich Nhat Hanh who said,

"TO BE beautiful means to be yourself. You don't need to be accepted by others. You need to accept yourself."

How do you accept yourself and relate to the world around you?

Concentrate on your strengths first and your weaknesses last. Take your focus away from what you don't like about yourself, or you will be unfairly pre-occupied by it. Instead, concentrate on the good things about you and they will grow. When acknowledging your strengths, you naturally reduce your occupation with the weaknesses you had, and you perform better in life. We all have weaknesses but if we focus on them, we lose our ability to operate from our very best performance.

- Speak well of yourself and others. Do not criticise, condemn or complain about yourself as people will view you in a negative way.
- Follow the rule that if you have nothing good to say, don't say anything at all.
- Look for the good in the world. Look for the good in other people and the positive actions they perform and compliment them for it.

Get Perspective by expanding your viewpoint and your options

Whenever you need to put life in perspective, look to the Universe around you. When you see that there is something bigger and more awe-inspiring than yourself, those little critical comparisons of what other people have, and what you don't, will begin to lose their significance. Know that you have strengths that they do not possess.

Put your health and wellbeing first, your loved ones next, and then decide where other people, animals, and the environment rank. If you don't put yourself first, you won't be able to effectively influence or inspire any other change in the world.

Organise and take pride in your life. Don't choose to live in chaos, because that means you are allowing the outside world to dictate most of your life. Live well first and don't wait for the right time to make a change, the only right time is to take some action now.

When relating and looking after yourself, this does not mean spoiling yourself by spending money you don't have, abusing yourself by indulging in your addictions beyond what you can handle, nor using or abusing others or the environment. It means ensuring your wellbeing, peace, and growth is nurtured. Many of the simplest and best pleasures in life are free and we now have more and more access to ideas, learning and visiting other parts of the world than any other time in history, through the internet.

Exercising in nature is a powerful way to take a break from our technical world of constant advertising and social media influencing. It gets you out from the four walls that occupies most of our existence. More and more people are turning away from gym memberships and exercising in their natural surroundings, including aerobic and strength training. Training outdoors takes a little creativity but it requires having very minimal equipment in your possession and is cheap compared to memberships or buying your own equipment. You can use trees, steps, rocks, public playground and public gyms to manage a significant workout.

Socially, seek people and groups from around the world who make you feel good. It is easier and easier to find your tribe through website social groups who share a similar philosophy or interest to you. However, it is also easier for very negative people to troll others on social media. That is their problem, and your solution is to rise above them and not get caught in their traps. They derive pleasure from people reacting to them. If trolling is an issue, it is better to seek more positive platforms to socialise that have strong administration monitoring powers to block the trolls.

Exercise 20: Creating Comfort in the Past

Nurture yourself gently.

1. Close your eyes and remember the sweet and innocent little child you once were.
2. Think of an event from your past when you were upset as a child. Imagine travelling back into the past to that event as the adult you are now.
3. Comfort that child you were with positive words of encouragement. Reassure them that everything will turn out alright and you are there to support them.
4. Let them know that they are a stronger person now through the many experiences they have had and lessons they have learned.
5. Give them a hug and leave them feeling supported and happy for the attention you have given them.
6. Quickly travel forward to the present, just like fast-forwarding a movie. As you travel, forgive yourself for any mistakes you have made along the way, dropping any burdens of guilt and remorse, shame and upset before you arrive in your present moment.
7. Gently ease out of the exercise.

YOU NEED to operate from this perfect moment and into the future in the best way you can, as there is no going back, at least not in our current science.

If you don't expect your family and friends to be perfect, don't expect that you can be too. We are human and we are flawed; it is part of our "human condition." Instead, celebrate the small wins of life. Don't deny them and act like a martyr who must suffer, or you will never appreciate the progress you have made so far.

YOU AND THOSE around you need the freedom to make their own decisions on how to live and who they choose to share their life with. It might mean that you, or they, decide you are not the right match. Though it can feel heartbreaking, it is the right choice in the long run. You should not want to feel the negative emotions that you are holding someone captive against their will for your own sake. People are not property. If you want the best for someone, as much as it hurts, let them go.

The author, poet and artist Kahlil Gibran wrote,

"IF YOU LOVE SOMEBODY, **let them go, for if they return, they were always yours. And if they don't, they never were."**

9

GRATEFULLY HAPPY

BEING MINDFUL OF WHAT YOU ALREADY HAVE AND GRATEFUL FOR WHAT LIFE GIVES

L iving with intention is a conscious practice that quickly connects you to appreciating the present moment. You begin to notice the beauty, shapes and symmetry of the world around you which takes you away from the mundanity of every day human commitments, trials and gossip. Being grateful for what you have already, comes through learning to detach yourself from circumstances which drain your attention and energy.

Our Universe is filled with awe and wonder. Noticing the patterns of nature in the clouds, the stars, a flower or a shell is a distinct contrast to the reality of our fast-paced and deadline-bound human world. Our attention is quickly absorbed by the overstimulation of information and the illusions created by media and advertising who profit from sensationalising the world around us. Being mindful is focusing on the now and appreciating your real existence from one-moment-to-the-next.

Worrying is a waste of time

Your life is not to be wasted on worrying about matters outside of your control and influence. If you worry, begin by changing your reaction to events. Just as in the earlier meditation practice in exercise 17, label your thoughts if they worry you and get in the habit of letting them pass by without judgement,

Simply say in your mind, "I accept you from a past that is no longer " or "I accept you as a future thought that hasn't happened," or simply label them "past" or "future."

Worry is the largest reason for practicing mindfulness. Worrying about your relationships, your job, the state of the world, and others' thoughts about you is a draining and wasteful activity. It drags you back into a past where you ruminate in circles about what you could have done or pulls you into a future which is just a negative prediction. Anyone who tells you that worrying is necessary or that it motivates you to action, have not thought about the time and emotion that has been invested on negative thinking when more effective positive thinking can be focused on instead. With a happy and optimistic attitude, you are already taking action as your focus is on the silver lining of that dark cloud of worry. A happy person looks for the seeds from which they will grow fruit.

We have to consider all the positive alternatives as an opportunity to set our minds to improving situations. Our life follows the rules that we make for ourselves. What we consistently focus on, and then act upon, determines what we will receive. "Kaizen" was discussed earlier in the book as the Japanese term which translates to "continuous improvement." It is within our need for survival to always improve our conditions. We continuously seek the positive improvement of our "Human Condition." Worrying is a signal to take action. When you first worry, you can dwell on it and then take action or you can immediately take action and limit that wasted "worry time."

When you start to worry, immediately ask,

- "What can I do right now to improve this?"

Step-by-step

By living mindfully, you take each moment a step at a time, and a step at a time is the best approach to handling any challenge. Writing word for word, running step by step, cooking instruction by instruction, and building brick by brick. This is our natural way of doing things.

Multi-tasking became a trend for quite a while but what it brought with it were more negatives than positives; such as, a lack of quality, a lack of detail, unfinished tasks, and the stress of overwhelm. Now, single-focus for human efficiency has once again come to the fore as customers expect quality products and services, and workers desire their wellbeing to be taken into consideration.

The trouble is when your mind is distracted by so much information, how do you reign in all your thoughts?

1. You begin by reducing your outside inputs.

   - *Close the door, the windows, the curtains or blinds and lock yourself away.*

2. You go back to focusing on one thing at a time. You turn off the distractions.

   - Close the necessary apps and windows on your phone, laptop or pc. *Change your music or radio station from vocal to instrumental, or work in quiet, white noise or nature sounds.*

3. You make sure your environment promotes peace and not interruption.

   - *Ensure you have everything ready before you start. Have your water or tea to hand, make sure you have planned for any tasks that will interrupt you, such as deliveries or appointments.*

4. You take a deep breath and calm yourself to a point where you dismiss all your thoughts and focus on your breathing right now.

- *Only have what you need to do directly in front of you. Place everything else out of your sight.*

5. Then you make a start. Take a 5 minute break and stretch your legs every 20 minutes.

- *20 minutes is about the time the average person can concentrate on a task for in one stretch, unless they are highly engrossed.*

The power of humour and a smile on your face

Humour is a route out of manageable pain that is an 8 or less out of 10 on your unhappiness scale explored in chapter 1. If you have the choice of wallowing in your sorrow or listening to some comedy about life, which do you choose? If you think you don't have a choice, guess what? Of course, you do!

Listen to and watch more humour over dark drama and tragedy. Humour will bring feelings of lightness and fun to your life. There are several types of humour that you can use spontaneously around others. Here are the main types:

- Wordplay: Twisting language for double-meaning or mixing a word up with another in the wrong way.
- Topical: Joking about things in popular society such as politicians or celebrities.
- Physical and absurd: Doing silly actions at random. Works great with kids, but also brings a quick laugh to many adults (possibly less so with serious intellectuals).
- Self-Deprecating: Often used by comedians to make light of their personal faults.
- Observational: Where you make light of everyday situations in life.

- Dark: Probably the least favourite as it requires reading a situation well to bring humour out of depressing situations and you don't know how others will react.

Humour that is physical, a play on words and observational are the most spontaneous, spur of the moment humour that we can create. If you are laughing, the only way you can cry at the same time is from laughter. Laughter releases the endorphins that we all need to reduce stress and feel happier. Endorphins are chemicals that the body produces to relieve pain and help raise a feeling of euphoria.

Exercise and endorphins

Exercise also releases endorphins. Exercise forces you to focus on the moment and raises your energy levels. When in the day, you start to feel yourself slipping into a grey fog or negative mood, one of the quickest ways to bring your energy back is to get in the habit of a quick one-minute workout or a number-based energy booster, such as jumping jacks for 1 minute or 20 jumping jacks. Choose what works best for you.

You may choose an upwards and outwards stretch instead or jog on the spot. The most important thing is to break your apathy by moving. Remember that Things Take Time, especially forming new habits which take consistency. Begin with short time frames which are easier to accomplish and reminders to get you to practice. Setting an alarm, notification reminder, entry in your digital device, smart speaker or a simple post-it notes in a space where you will see it, will help you to keep this new habit in mind.

If you are working for 20 minutes slots, use a minutes exercise as a part of your 5 minute break.

Appreciating the wonders of everyday life

The world is a special place, and we can find remarkable experiences all around us. Pick up any object nearby and think of its design and the process of how it came into existence, look at the sky and notice how many subtle colours are in it. Everything is special, there is a wonder to life, we just need to get back to being in awe of it. Look to the Universe and put things in perspective.

If you are bored or you feel nothing excites you anymore, force yourself to stop for a moment and show some respect for the infinite detail and limitlessness of everything around you! Look, really look at the tiniest thing to hand or look out at the vastness of the night's sky. Don't take life for granted or your perspective will dull and so too will your personality.

You have no reason to take anything for granted. You have just been indulging in the smallest view of life with yourself at the centre. You need to look outwards away from the petty day-to-day social and cultural norms.

To be happy, you don't need to possess things to admire them. Often when we get what we think we want, we become desensitised to having them and look for our next possession. It is often better to admire from afar, than possess it and end up disappointed.

You cannot possess everything you want; it is simply not healthy to have that physical and mental weight of responsibility for stuff. Everything you own requires care and maintenance. If it burdens you and weighs you down, it is time to let it go. You feel better when you have a clearer, cleaner space in which to enjoy the experiences that life brings. You lose opportunities for real life experiences when you become pre-occupied with your stuff and the time consumed maintaining it, or the energy and thought spent pursuing the things you don't yet possess.

The Natural World

Why are we so fascinated by the invention of a new plastic or the unboxing of new products on YouTube? We are surrounded by a declining environment where plastic is poisoning our waters and trees are plants are being decimated. Several species are becoming extinct every single year, never to be seen again in nature.

Where is our focus?

Many of us have lost touch with an appreciation for nature and chosen a people-constructed focus on living in an artificial world. We need to make conscious choices for what supports the natural world over what destroys it. What we invest in grows:

- Invest in greed and you will never be satisfied as there is always something more to possess at the expense of the environment, animals and other people.
- Invest in anger, blame and hurting others and your enemies will grow as will your negative contribution to society in general.
- Invest in negativity and you will spiral downwards into upset, misery and cynicism.

- Invest in caring and being mindful and you will support the environment, animals and other people.
- Invest in happiness and you will attract likeable people.
- Invest in positivity and you will contribute to the social improvement of our world.
- Invest in appreciation and you will see the awe of the Universe, especially in the simplest of things.

Gratefulness and harmony

Gratefulness is the route to peace. You do not have to impress anyone, and you aren't here to force your views upon others. By being grateful, you are respecting life. Good actions follow on from gratefulness allowing a positive flow of energy to influence all around you.

Resistance to the flow of energy can be the result of anger, hate, and other negative feelings that become blocked inside. Eventually, these feelings emotionally explode or weep out from you.

Life is a delicate balance and if we can keep some harmony in our lives, we are contributing to bettering our world. Others will choose to contribute to the exploitation and destruction of the world for their selfish short-term power and greed. It is a conscious choice on the part of every individual.

Relax into the moment and focus on what positive action you can take now. As you consciously practice harmonious ways of interacting with others, you will begin to unconsciously develop this positive habit. You will be a conduit for good energy to flow through you and others will enjoy being in your company.

We should all exercise some caution when we first meet other people as they are strangers and we know nothing yet about them; however, a smile or a friendly "Hi" will never go amiss. Be grateful for those precious people in your life and your chance to meet new and interesting friends and associates.

Inspire others by living gratefully

Finding fault should never dominate your thinking and most of your actions should be invested on improvement. The good must outweigh the bad if we are to lead a happier life.

When you are in the company of someone blocking the flow of positive energy with their negative thinking, your best path is to refuse to join them in their outlook. You need to model a higher level of experiencing the world, for your wellbeing and theirs.

This does not mean confronting them about their negativity. Confrontation leads to defensiveness and resistance. You model a better way of living by remaining positive in your thoughts and actions, noticing the good things, and being grateful for the opportunities around you. You demonstrate how to take advantage of the opportunities by experiencing them yourself.

Offer them the opportunity to join you without expectations that they will. If they don't, you still go and enjoy those opportunities. Don't sacrifice an opportunity for someone who refuses to join in, just to please them. They will notice the benefit of your experiences and one day may join you; if they don't, that is their choice.

By indirectly role-modelling a better, more positive way to live, your friend, family member, colleague or student may take on your habits or seek advice from you. This may be because they are ready for a change or because they can see the success the approach is making in your life. It may be a conscious decision on their part or an unconscious response just by being around you.

You can directly promote the simple benefits of changing a behaviour by working together. The following techniques are used in coaching and guiding others to make a positive change. I have used an example of someone recovering from an accident and getting back into exercise after receiving medical advice and exercise approval from their Doctor. If you are seeking a change related to health or a medical condition, always get approval from your Medical Specialist first and a specific programme to follow.

1. Encouraging their dreams with a vision of a better future without their current problem.

"Next year we could go on that hiking holiday we've always dreamed of if we start to get fit and do some day walks now. Let's plan a walk for Saturday."

2. Addressing their fears with reassuring responses.

"I know you are worried about your fitness, that's why we are doing this together. We will start gently and for a short length of time and gradually extend our walks. By this time next year, you will be fitter than you have been for a long while."

3. Understanding their failures with the promise that you will be there to listen to them.

"I know that you gave up on exercise a few years ago because of your accident. The Doctor has said that you need to be more active and moderate aerobic exercise is the best thing to improve your recovery and fitness."

4. Clarifying the simple steps along the path to achieve the goal with measurable numbers and deadlines.

"The Doctor has given us this programme to follow, so let's break it down into achievable steps. This week we will be walking every day for about 20 minutes at a pace where we can still carry on a conversation without being out of breath. We can stop at any point and rest if you feel breathless or experience any pain."

How your unconscious can help you to be more mindful

One of the best ways to be mindful and simplify our lives is to get in touch with our unconscious for problem-solving. It may sound mystical, but it actually naturally occurs in our everyday lives.

You are mulling over a problem and later a solutions or solutions come to mind. For example, you are wondering how to best reply to an angry email from a customer and your first draft is too confrontational. While you sleep on it, you unconsciously search for words and phrases to write a better email. The next day, you review your reply in a more understanding, constructive and helpful way to benefit the customer and your business.

If we consciously give our unconscious a question that it can solve without our conscious interference, it can be surprising what ideas we come up within moments throughout the day . Say you want to decide which colour to paint your kitchen wall. If you ask this question before you go to sleep, your unconscious will likely continue to think of all the possibilities of which colour will work as they play out in your imagination. The next morning, you have a good idea of what colour will work best aesthetically and practically.

Why ask a question before sleeping?

Sleep can be a great time for our unconscious mind to work on finding solutions because your conscious mind is more relaxed and less critical and interfering. If you find that this interferes with your sleep, try asking your question first thing in the morning. I personally find that some of my best ideas come when I am in an automatic physical routine, such as having a shower or walking. Mindfully asking the power of the unconscious mind for answers to questions can lead to better answers that match your inner feelings and beliefs.

Exercise 21: Your Own Personal Guru

One exercise I like to practice when I am looking for an answer to a question is a visualisation I do just before I go to sleep.

1. Imagine climbing a steep mountain toward the clouds. It is a difficult journey and takes time and effort.
2. When you get to the top, amongst the clouds you come across a beautifully ornate, hidden temple.
3. Outside of the temple is a piece of parchment and a feather quill (pen) with an ink pot on a plinth, upon which you write the question you are seeking an answer for.
4. Once you have written your question, you ring a rope-pull bell and wait. Eventually a solemn-looking monk opens the doors to collect the question and takes it inside, closing the doors behind them. You are left waiting once again outside the closed doors.
5. When the answer is ready you hear a bell, the temple doors are opened, and you are asked to enter.
6. In a vast room, you walk toward a seated single wise person or if you wish, a wise panel of guides.
7. With some ceremony, they deliver their insightful and constructive answer to you.
8. You thank them for their answer and leave, with the door closing tightly behind you, feeling excited by all the possibilities as you make your way back down the mountain.

THE SIMPLE STRUCTURE of this exercise mirrors that of a story. It starts with a difficult journey which takes time and effort because you value finding the answer to the question for which you seek. Once you reach your destination, you find a way to consciously pose your question to your unconscious mind. Your unconscious is represented by a panel or a single figure who you value or trust with an answer.

This someone may be a hero, celebrity, famous deceased person or anyone you respect and consider an authority in the area you are seeking an answer for. You might ask questions about how they do what you wish to do; for example, you might ask Beyonce how she produces such an easy, melodic voice, or you might ask Oprah how she remains so inspired and positive. The representative figure is simply an engagement of your unconscious to come up with some answers in line with your beliefs and the values that best benefit you. When you receive your answer, you thank the figure or group representing your unconscious.

Drop your Ego by looking outwards to others and nature.

When presenting yourself to the outside world, you place yourself in the likely position of selling, defending or justifying your opinions, appearance and actions. This is a part of life, and you must uphold your beliefs if they benefit yourself and others by improving a situation or reasserting human rights.

When however, you stubbornly force yourself and your beliefs upon others, your ego has taken over. An ego of self-importance and self-validation is communicating messages such as,

"IT'S ALL ABOUT ME."
   "I'm right, you're wrong!"
   "I make the decisions and you follow."
   "I am in control."

FUNCTIONING from pure ego is not giving, improving or showing gratitude to those around you. To give you a clear example of ego-driven personalities, you just need to look at those in dictatorial positions. Often they operate from a social and personality disorder and lack empathy, at the expense of those under their rules. They are dominating and controlling. They will defend their position with strong defiance, even when they are under pressure to leave.

In normal life, there are many levels of ego in the people you encounter in your life.

How do you recognise when your ego is involved in your interactions with others?

- Justifying or defending any actions you execute without taking others' views into consideration.
- Justifying or defending anything you have said without listening to what other people have to say.
- Getting upset by perceived or real criticism and blaming other people for the response.
- Refusing to accept that other people have rights too.
- Refusing to accept the natural world and its events as integral to human life.
- Refusing to accept consequences for your actions and inactions.

The impact of the words we speak

Most of what is said in the world are words only and rarely result in any need for action. In our personal lives the words that impact us the most are the negative words that other people say in reference to us, usually in the form of insults and gossip. These words unbalance our ego and break our trust, upsetting us through the perceived negative intent behind them. How do we remain positive when we feel under attack?

We have to let go of the feeling that it is personal, even when we know it was deliberate. Often there is a hidden agenda behind these words to somehow benefit the person who spoke them, therefore their harmful words may not be commensurate with the gain they receive. The other party may well have wanted you to respond emotionally to get a certain reaction from you.

- Maybe they feel there is a very good reason to do so; maybe you haven't been clear or paid them attention, have hurt them in some way or they feel you don't deserved something because you haven't earned it.
- Maybe they are attempting to assert their power in the company of others.
- Maybe they have been hurt themselves and are projecting their hurt outward anyway they can.
- Maybe they are mean-spirited and enjoy the pleasure of hurting other people as an internal negativity and cynicism and possible psychological issue.

HOWEVER, whatever their justification, it would be more reasonable if they were transparent about their desired need. Sometimes this behaviour is an unconscious pattern of behaviour on their part and they are not even aware of it.

No matter what their intention or reasons, listen. Words are often held deep in the unconscious and they can play out in our minds for years to come. A defensive response to what they say will create conflict, more upset, or their further pleasure. Listen and maybe you can help the situation by recognising their intention and responding in an emotionally even and measured way,

"I hear what you are saying, however I'd prefer you told me exactly what you want in words that were not so personal so that maybe I can help."

VIEWING PAST UPSETS FROM AN OBJECTIVE, rather than subjective, perspective can help you clarify the intentions of criticisms. If someone has made you feel the victim by their bullying, it is a result of their own needs to feel better about themselves. It is their problem that they are trying to resolve in the wrong way. As difficult as it is, it's time to forgive their actions and begin to be grateful for where you are now in your life. You are you and are leading your own life now without the need for their misguided influence.

Make the effort to take something positive from the experience, no matter how long it takes.

For example:

- Your boss may have fired you unfairly.
- *You are grateful that this was the wrong person to continue working for and you will find a more conducive workplace for your efforts.*
- Your partner says they are leaving you as they don't love you in the same way anymore.
- *You are grateful that you are not stuck in a relationship with someone who no longer shares your love and you will find someone who will.*
- Your medical specialist tells you that you have the early signs of health issues and you have to make drastic changes in your lifestyle to stay well.
- *You are grateful that you have been given a warning and have a chance to improve your health.*

When you drop ego-driven responses, accept what is happening and then mindfully make choices, you allow emotional energy to flow through you, rather than resisting and erupting in an explosion of pent-up emotions. Upset and anger, although natural responses, are not the conscious choice for a person living a positive and happy life. A person living a happy and positive life will listen and choose proactive responses to improve their situation.

When you are feeling happy and positive in your acceptance of "what is," you have no need to excuse your negative responses, because you haven't chosen them in the first place.

Gaining perspective through the wonders of our Universe

Everything in our Universe is made from particles of energy. The atoms that make up our world can only be viewed under an electron or helium microscope in clusters. To put that in perspective, it is estimated that 1 to 10 million atoms could fit on a pinhead, depending on the type of atom. An atom is not even the tiniest element we know. If the nucleus of an atom was represented as a grain of sand, an atom itself would be about 150 metres in width. The splitting of a few atoms atoms can create enough fission energy to cause a nuclear explosion.

Our Universe came into existence from no place and no time, known as the "Big Bang." All we see and all that is unseen came from possibly nothing or at least very few particles, yet it is now so vast and complex and is our "everything." The Universe is the result of an absolute "miracle" beyond our human thinking. From the tiniest speck to the largest astral body, there is nothing that we cannot be fascinated by.

With the power of your unconscious mind to run your body and the millions of cells that make up your body, we have our own Universe within our very brain, running at a sub-atomic level. You are in the lucky position to choose your experiences and reactions from one moment to the next. You are creating life in every choice you make.

Let go of your worries, your disappointments and your fears. Embrace using your imagination, your ability to look for the positive and the happiness you can find from just appreciating the smallest little pleasures that are always around you. Don't take it for granted, be grateful.

Managing the tragedies of life

When life tragedies occur and put you into a state of crises, the only way to handle them is one step at a time, from moment to moment.

As you try and process the event, you will be dragged into the recent past or pulled into a future of thoughts that are not yet a reality.

Being overwhelmed by deep emotions means that you will have difficulty focusing. If you have problems to handle, handle them in the moment and they will become more manageable. If you continue to be pulled into future fears, ask realistically,

"What is the worst that can happen now?"

Know that no matter what is to come, things will improve, that pain will pass, and grief will lessen. No experience, no matter how traumatic at the time, will continue for ever. Be brave and bear through it. Cling to a glimmer of hope.

You are alive now, and you have managed to survive up until this point. You are stronger and more resilient than you think. Your evolution as a human has ensured that you positively fight to survive in even the most difficult of circumstances or surrender yourself to letting go when absolutely no other options are available. The first law of thermodynamics in a simplified form states that,

ENERGY CANNOT BE CREATED **nor destroyed, only transformed.**

Exercise 22: Practicing Gratefulness

1. In the morning, think of three simple things you will likely be grateful for today.
2. When you go to bed, think of three simple things you were grateful for experiencing today.

This is how you establish a positive pattern of happiness in your life each and every day.

If you just can't think of anything or a bad experience has overwhelmed your thinking, ask:

. . .

"WHAT ONE THING can I learn from this bad experience that can be used constructively?"

Simple pleasures

Show your gratefulness by enjoying and recognising your simple pleasures. Simple pleasures can make your day a happy experience. Here are 50 ideas for simple pleasures:

1. A clear desk and working space
2. A warm or fresh breeze
3. A mindful morning walk or jog
4. A fine dessert
5. A great read
6. A hike in the surrounding beauty of nature
7. A meaningful conversation with a close friend
8. Admiring the stars and the moon in the night sky
9. An empty inbox in your email
10. A classic old or new release movie
11. An uncluttered room to rest in
12. Being lazy on a Sunday after a busy week
13. Making bubble mixture and blowing bubbles
14. Completing a task on your to-do list
15. Cuddling a loved one or your pet
16. Indulging in a piece of chocolate
17. Drawing and colouring
18. Enjoying the sound of rain while keeping cosy
19. Floating in a pool
20. Cooking and enjoying fresh-baked treats
21. Having or giving a massage
22. Sharing a family picnic in nature
23. Helping someone out
24. Listening to good music, singing, dancing and letting go
25. Being affectionate and making Love
26. Putting a smile on someone's face

27. Playing in a sandpit with you children or grandchildren
28. Pushing your child or grandchildren on a swing, or even your partner!
29. Saving your small change and watching it grow
30. Listening to your favourite podcast, an audible book or radio station
31. Sitting or lying on the grass and looking up at the drifting clouds
32. Snowball fights and snowy fun
33. Staring into the embers and flames of a fireplace
34. Taking a long relaxing shower or bath
35. Indulging in an afternoon nap on the sofa
36. Tea, Coffee or a nice hot chocolate
37. Sharing jokes and riddles with someone
38. The feeling after good exercise
39. Mowing the lawn and enjoying the look and smell of freshly cut grass
40. Playing a board game with your children, family or friends
41. Appreciating a clean and clear home
42. Walking barefoot on a sandy beach
43. Squelching through mud and puddles in waterproof boots
44. Seeing animals in nature
45. Listening to and enjoying the ocean, a stream or pond
46. Watching a sunrise or sunset
47. Enjoying your children or grandchildren playing
48. Seeing your kids play sport
49. Writing down your thoughts, ideas or reflections
50. Practicing yoga, stretching, tai chi, or meditation

GRATITUDE AND PLEASURE

When you experience true love, the best of yourself is reflected back to you. When you have a moment of deep love, you are fully in that moment. It is a euphoria that awakens you into the present. A feeling of touch from that other person is precious, pleasurable and comforting. It is a connection you want to last for as long as you possibly can. You are feel the full flow of energy as it passes through you without resistance.

Although feelings and emotions are transitory, you do not need to spend big money each time you want to experience a euphoric moment of pleasure. Simple pleasures can make your day just by indulging in them for a moment in time. The warmth of the tea in your mug, the sight of beautiful colours in that sunset, the feeling of a warm breeze and the sound it produces through the trees, and the reflection in a puddle. All these things can create moments of wonder for free, several times a day.

Buying a car, jewellery, clothing, drinking, taking drugs may give you a momentary high, but unlike the free, simple pleasures in life, they come with a cost to your health, wellbeing and financial status.

THE PRESENT MOMENT is where things matter. It is where you will find positivity and feel happiest. Can we always live in the moment? We can certainly have more moments by consciously enjoying the simple things as a practice. You need to feel good now, not by thinking of past events, nor waiting until your fantasy desire has finally arrived in your life. We live along a linear timeline made of present moments. Why sacrifice a 'present' moment with negative thoughts about the past or future.

Nothing you physically possess will last. You buy that amazing thing one moment and then in another moment of it being amazing is gone in a flash. You win the lottery, Hooray! The euphoria goes by in a flash. You win that Oscar! The moment of winning and achieving is gone before you know it. That is why being rich or successful is no guarantee of happiness or even improving it. Happy and positive people don't win big, they win small, many times through the day. They come from all walks of life and enjoy what is before them right now. There is no over-indulgence in the past or wasted thoughts of the future.

. . .

IF ALL YOU dream about is an amazing future and waste your 'present' moment doing so, you miss the moments of opportunity to bring yourself closer to that future. The future is a trap for wishful thinkers. Instead, take action and choose to experience the future feeling you want right now. After all, everything we do and get is to attain a feeling, nothing more, and as feelings are not materialistically attained your choice is simple. Experience the now and be grateful for what you already have.

QUESTION:

- What do you want to be when you grow up?

Answer:

- I am already all I want to be, happy, as I continue enjoying this present moment.

10

POSITIVE MONEY, HAPPY BUSINESS
MONEY DOESN'T CHANGE PEOPLE, IT ONLY HIGHLIGHTS
WHO THEY ACTUALLY ARE

M oney doesn't discriminate as to who possesses it. It doesn't have the consciousness to care who owns it. An unscrupulous person may have a lot of it and many good people might not have much at all.

Being rich is relative. Compare a poorer third world household next to a first world household, next to a millionaire household, next to a billionaire household. Who is rich in the eyes of the poorer third world household and who is rich in the eyes of the millionaire household?

Despite the different divisions of wealth in the world, we can all share the many other kinds of rich experiences, from close friends and family to the beauty of nature. Is the wealthy person who stresses over protecting and managing their finances and position in a better place than the poorer person struggling financially but grateful and appreciative of what they do have?

Sometimes having less means having more.

IT IS important to work with what you have, rather than what you don't. You have to say,

"This is what we are working with. This is the asset pile and this is the deficit pile. Let's focus on the assets, because the deficit isn't going to do us any good. Now, how are we going to build upon it?"

Money is relative

For many years, people have exclaimed, "I wish I was a millionaire." There is something about the million figure that seems to evoke having successfully made it financially. It is a label that states if you have a million, everything is okay. It is a relative number. A million pounds GBP is different to a million US or a million rupees. Money is more about what will maintain your comfort levels in the moment and what you can save for your future if you are no longer earning money. Your comfort levels will change throughout life as will the value of the pound, dollar and rupee. It is all about what you value in your life or what the market values.

The value of a tiny one-bedroom flat in the city may be worth the value of a whole 4 or 5 bedroom house, or even two, in a small town.

I know how important money is to live comfortably, but living comfortably means different things for different people. As a happy and optimistic person there is no need to wait to be in possession of a certain amount of money before choosing to live with happiness and positivity. There is no reason for money to make you happy.

If you work in a highly stressful environment, in a position that you dislike and with little time for you own interests and passions, you might be considering changing your job or career. If in that job you are working for money alone at the detriment of your physical and mental health, know that there are always other options. to balance your work and leisure time. Mental and physical health is more important than any money you amass.

Money might increase your feelings of security, but there is no security in the poor health you could earn through stress, mental and physical wear and tear in your pursuit of money. Healthier security might be found in an area with more affordable housing and better living conditions while seeking a job with less pressure. Money is relative to the limits of what possessions and lifestyle you think you need and want. Reducing your spending on needs and wants, means more money in your bank account.

If you want to manage your money better, learn to be sparing. Just as in a game of cards, you don't reveal your hand until the end, the same goes with your money. If you want the whole pizza, cake or packet of cookies eaten in one go, by all means place it on the table, and watch it be consumed. If you want it to last, spread out the time of its consumption, place it on the table a portion at a time.

When everything is in front of us, it is too tempting to not indulge until there is nothing left. For some it's all too overwhelming. The same goes for money. Put aside a fixed amount to spend after each pay, only after you have put aside some savings first, followed by your bills.

The best way to grow your finances is to save a certain percentage of your income immediately on being paid via an automatic transfer or your discipline to manually transfer the money. If you don't earn much, still put a tiny amount aside first. If you earn a lot, put a big slice into your savings. You would be surprised how many people who earn much more than you have no savings at all. Saving is not a product of earning more money, it is a product of discipline.

If you begin earning a little or a lot more, you will have established the discipline of saving to increase your contributions. At least try and follow the 80/20 Pareto rule. Put at least 20% of your money aside as a minimum and find creative ways to live on the rest if it is still a struggle for you.

For those who say, yes but I like to enjoy life and life costs money, only extravagant pleasures are costly. The simpler enjoyments like family, friends and exercise don't have to cost you anything.

Many people choose to never pay full price for anything. A close friend of mine wears the most amazing designer clothes and she works in a modestly paid administration role. She has taste and she has style. Her clothes come at little cost as she shops in charity shops, waiting patiently for clothes of the right type to come in. These clothes cost the original owner many times more than she pays.

Some she has bought were never even worn in the first place before being donated. The secret to her style is that she knows the colours and cuts that suit her best, which she learned by reading books about the clothing style programme, "Color Me Beautiful."

Having a money mind

Like attracts like and though it is no guarantee, if money is your focus, how you think and behave with it now is likely a reflection of whether you have it or lack it. Some people view having money as greedy or selfish and therefore they are likely not to have it in their hands for long, as they will unconsciously find ways to be rid of the discomfort of having it.

This is an unconscious behaviour from a belief or value they hold, likely formed in a time of their life when they learned to associate money with some kind of pain: actual, perceived or taught by another. The simple rule is that if you spend your money, it will fall into the hands of someone else as money, like any other energy, continues to flow when you let it go.

People with an understanding around money, find the best ways to multiply it. As they focus on it, save it and invest it, the money grows. Like all aspects of your life, if you feel secure and comfortable with something, you will attract more of the same. If you feel uncomfortable, you are going to find ways to not have it in your life. If you operate from discomfort, after you have met your basic needs, your excess money will usually being spent on something that does not grow in value, like leisure and pleasure. The old belief that "To make money takes money," is true. Even if you built up your money from nothing, if you don't utilise its power to grow, it will leave you and pass on to someone else.

Money and creativity

Do you have to be a businessperson to make money?
Do you have to be cold and ruthless?

We tend to see the exciting, high adrenaline Gordon Gecko approach to making money as seen in the movies "Wall street" and the real-life rise to riches story of Jordan Belfort in "The Wolf of Wolf Street." These movies portray greed, corruption and the spoils of excess money and the final downfall of the protagonist.

As pointed out earlier, money does not discriminate. If it is not gained through theft, it is there for whoever finds the best ways of being given it by other people. Managing it and growing it takes learned skill, just like any other skill.

Having worked with a number of people who have built successful businesses, I have seen that they might not have started with a money mindset, but as their business grew, they quickly had to pick up the skills as they went along. Many of the businesspeople I conversed with were creatively-minded; including designers, inventors and entrepreneurs. They initially had a vision for something that would serve others and were then driven to give birth to their idea. They also had a fair amount of empathy to know what people would want or need.

Their compelling vision moved them through the obstacles that others with less compelling visions would eventually give up on. The most important trait I noticed was their general positivity and happiness for having chosen to pursue their dreams, even in the early and more challenging times. Their energy levels were high.

What lies at the base of creative entrepreneurship is the ability to transfer what is in your imagination to something that inspires a customer to want to spend their money on that product or service.

How you get money

You can grow your money in a number of ways. Here are a few:

- By creating more income from your product or service gaining in demand and popularity.
- Buying something and improving it and then selling it on.

- Renting or leasing out something that you own or are renting and leasing yourself (where allowed).
- Lending your money to others and receiving interest.

Exercise 23: What Have I Got to Give?

If you are looking for ideas to build a business on the side to generate some income, ask yourself:

- "What skills can I offer that others might benefit from?"
- "What personal strengths do I have that others might benefit from?"
- "What do I really like doing that I would continue to enjoy even if it became a business?"
- "What is something unique that I can do that people will pay me to deliver as a product or service?"
- "What is something I have always desired to learn that would earn me some money?"
- "If I choose this path of making money, how will it effect my happiness?

Spreading the word of what you have to offer

Of course, for your business to grow, you need to get words and images of what you do out to the world. A couple of years ago (before the writing of this book) I had a discussion with a Lead Public Relations and Advertising Managers from the London advertising and communications agency "Saatchi and Saatchi" about the most effective way to get your product known.

She said that you always need a good story behind your product. People buy more on the perceived experience the product offers more than the product itself. Whether the story is true or a work of fiction, people relate to the character in that fiction identifying with and/or admiring the character's strong feelings and the actions they take. Individuals look to a possible positive lifestyle that they can aspire to achieve. Once a story is established, a compelling visual image is designed that immediately captures the feeling of that story and relates it to a modern audience following current trends.

Other tips that were given to me, were to go the extra mile beyond what your competitors offer, and to only make promises that you can deliver on.

This marketing approach applies to the many areas of our lives where we wish to inspire, rather than demand change in other people and systems. From Greta Thunberg, David Attenborough, and Elon Musk, they all have compelling stories and messages behind what they do, which we pay attention to. This also applies to us in our personal development. Our selling point is the fact that we all have a backstory that is unique, individual and has shaped who we are today.

What are the points of interest and strengths of your backstory?

WITH THE ADVENT of online social media, and with the time and effort, you can bring attention to your products with little to no finances. Google, Amazon, eBay and easy website creators such as Wix and Squarespace offer easy setups and instant markets. Once you have established yourself on a platform, to draw traffic, you have to become familiar with using Keywords to attract the right audience from the billions of people on the internet.

If you want to have a positive impact on the world, add news-worthy value to your business by asking the following key questions as your business grows:

- "How can I make this even more ethical or environmentally conscious?"
- "How can I do even more with less ......?"
- "How can I increase efficiency to use less resources?"
- "Who exactly are my customers and what lifestyles do they lead?"
- "Where will I find my customers?"

- "What words would my customers use to search and find my products on the internet?"
- "How can I spread the word and meet more customers?"
- "How can I get feedback from customers to improve what I am offering?"
- "How can I show how much I appreciate my customers?"
- "How can I show how much I appreciate my staff?"
- "How can I go the extra mile to help my customers/staff?"
- "How can I deliver my product or service in an environmentally friendly way?"

Exercise 24: Money Magnet

Develop a commitment to being involved in the money process and its importance to your life.

1. In a dissociated view, see yourself looking at your bank statement with a positive amount of money as the total, free of debt.

- How do you feel about being debt free?
- What amount of money do you notice in your account?
- Why do you think you are seeing this particular amount?
- Would you prefer to see more?

2. Now see yourself as financially independent.

- How do you feel?
- What are you wearing?
- What are your surroundings?

3. Imagine that you are attracting a steady stream of money toward yourself. Allow it to flow through you and some of it to continue onward.

- What have you opened up to the world to attract this money?
- What exact skill set have you learned to attract this money toward you?
- What product or service do you offer that is so popular to others that they are giving you their money to purchase it?

4. Visualise yourself in a happy mood as you think about the money and assets in your life.

- What would a successful relationship with money feel like?
- What would the right amount of assets look like? (What would you have? What would you no longer have?)
- What would you need to learn to understand money better?
- What would you need to do to feel more comfortable with money? (learn about taxes, learn about saving or investing etc.)

11

HEALTH AND HAPPINESS
THE GREATEST WEALTH IS HEALTH

To keep ourselves existing for as long as possible, we must maintain our personal health physically and mentally. One very simple health rule to follow is the teaching of IBM programmer George Fuechsel, the "GIGO" acronym, meaning Garbage In, Garbage Out. GIGO, was originally modelled for computer coding around input and output. If you input a programme with garbage, you will get an output of garbage in return. This model is easily applicable to our human lifestyles. We can eat garbage food, and input other garbage substances into our body, lie around like a sack of garbage, and think garbage thoughts, and our output for doing so will be the consequences of the garbage we originally input.

Body and mind signals

Your body and thoughts consistently give signals that alert you to changes you need to take to maintain your health and wellbeing. When your body experiences pain, it is signalling that there is a problem needing attention, either very soon or immediately, depending on its intensity. When your body aches and strains or you experience fatigue, it is a signal that you need to rest and recuperate.

When your thoughts cause you pain, hurt or anxiety, it is a signal that you need to give them some positive attention to alleviate them. Your thought pain will be worrying about a past situation or a worry about a future-focused event that hasn't occurred.

Thought pain is best managed by focusing on what you have control of right now and letting go of what you don't. With the ability to control and change your thoughts and reactions, first identify the accompanying feeling; if you feel guilt or shame, forgive yourself and assure yourself that you have changed and it's unlikely to happen again.

You are flawed as all humans are, and you cannot be perfect all of the time. If your guilt and shame are causing pain or hurt to someone else, you need to find ways to make amends. A sincere apology is a very good start. If your thoughts are giving you a warning about a future event, it is either your fears creating anxiety or a message that you need to do things in a different way in order to improve the chance of it not manifesting. Most of what we worry about in the future does not actually happen.

Pain is a call to action. Fear is the imaginary obstacle that holds you back from taking action in the first place. As the popular saying goes, fear is,

<u>F</u>alse
<u>E</u>vidence
<u>A</u>ppearing
<u>R</u>eal

US PRESIDENT FRANKLIN D Roosevelt said,

"THE ONLY THING we have to fear is fear itself."

WE SHOULD NOT BE afraid of pain and we should always follow through when we experience it. If you are taken to hospital because of pain signalling that there is something wrong, then it is the best place for you to improve your situation.

Imagine if you didn't experience pain. There are people who have a congenital insensitivity to pain, and they are in danger of life-threatening problems as a result of not receiving pain signals after accidents. If you did not experience pain from serious cuts, broken bones, burns or issues with internal organs, the chance of your survival could lessen.

Beware of self-sabotage

if you have ever given up quickly on that healthy eating or exercise program, you might be experiencing the unconscious positive intention behind self-sabotage. One reasons that people self-sabotage is a lack of self-esteem. Feelings of worthlessness and the belief that you don't deserve success may have an unconscious intention of keeping you comfortable or not putting you in the position of humiliating yourself in front of others. Some people may self-sabotage because it makes them feel in control of their situation when they feel that they are unable to control other aspects of their life. The unconscious intention is clearly to have some element of control in life, even if it's bad.

Until your very last breath, you can do your best to keep your body serving you well through exercise, healthy eating and positive thinking. If you are deliberately sabotaging your body through bad lifestyle choices, be grateful that you can change right now when you have got to the bottom of the unconscious intention behind your behaviour.

Appreciate that there are many other people whose physical and intellectual performance has been affected since birth or due to accidents and illness. There is always someone out there wishing they could have at least your physical capability as they are functioning with less. There are also many inspiring people living with physical and intellectual challenges who focus on what they can do with what they have, making positive choices, enjoying life and being happy.

Being happy and maintaining your positivity helps you to manage the stresses and stressors that we know can damage our physical and mental health.

The holistic approach

Think of your body, mind and consciousness as a whole. Every part of you is interlinked in a balance working for wellness. There is always a battle going on inside our body as we fight invaders and rogue cells. Mentally, we must be vigilant against rogue thoughts. When battles are being lost, our health declines and we need to help our bodies recuperate by reducing added external stress and resting.

What we put into our bodies, how we exercise the muscle of our heart and the muscles of our body, and how we manage to keep our thoughts calm are all entwined and impact upon our whole self. Being positive and happy helps promote the health of our body. Laughter or humour are often called best medicine. Amongst the health benefits of happiness are better sleep, feeling less stress, and having lower blood pressure.

Ancient Greek Philosopher Epictetus said,

Holistic exercise for the body and mind

Once you have sought approval to enter an exercise programme from your Doctor, ways to improve your physical and mental wellbeing are daily:

- Stretching and weight bearing exercises which improves the flexible range and strength of your body. Activities include sports stretching and yoga, body weight, machine or free weights.

- Cardiac activity which improves the strength of your heart muscle. Cycling, swimming, running, dancing or any other activity that raises your heart rate for a period of time. The general advice is:

1. Warm up for 10 minutes with light aerobic exercise that is a reflection of your activity such as gentle cycling, walking, swimming, or movement.
2. Sustain aerobic exercise for 20 to 30 minutes at a level where you are still able to carry on a conversation with someone else.
3. Finally, cool down until your heart rate has dropped to its average daily beats per minute. For most people this is around 60 to 70 beats per minute.

- Meditation, moving meditation such as Tai Chi, or the active mental process of self-hypnosis improves the thoughts you have as you relax. As you let go, accept the thoughts and allow the energy of acceptance to pass freely through you. Other mindful activities such as reading, cooking, colouring, knitting, puzzles or other single-focused hobbies are also beneficial.

ALL OF THESE holistic elements help release the following natural chemicals encouraging happy feelings:

- Endorphins: Which is a chemical pain reducer, released after exercise, also relieving stress and anxiety.
- Serotonin: Which is a mood stabiliser released by exercise, eating, sunlight and exercise. It can make you feel more confident, regulates your sleep, and improves memory and sexual desire.
- Dopamine: Released during pleasurable experiences, enhancing motivation, determination, learning and pleasure.

- Oxytocin: Released during sex, giving us feelings of trust to build our relationship.

THE QUICKEST NATURAL routes to releasing "Feel Good" chemicals are:

- Continuous exercise
- Laughter
- Meditation
- Listening to music
- Sex
- Dark Chocolate
- Creating art, writing, music
- Dancing
- Massage
- TV, film, theatre, sport and concerts which stirs your emotions.
- Wine

EVERYTHING IN MODERATION, of course.

12

FINDING MEANING THROUGH HAPPY LIVING
THE MEANING OF LIFE IS TO GIVE YOUR LIFE MEANING

"Happiness is the meaning and the purpose of life, the whole aim and end of human existence."
Aristotle, Ancient Greek philosopher

WE ARE CONTINUOUSLY LEARNING and adapting. It is a part of our nature to survive. There is always much to learn and so many opportunities to apply our learning in the real world. Our lives present us with a never-ending supply of new experiences, some good and some seemingly bad. What we do with this learning is really down to our choices. Happy and positive people are more inclined to practice what they have learned without hesitation, whereas those with a critically negative mindset will air caution over risk and change. You may have noticed that when you don't learn from an experience and find a better way to deal with a challenge, it will appear again and again until you do take notice and positive action. We are lucky to have these repeating signals to remind us of our need to change.

Life is a journey of learning

Taking any action in life, even in relation to something you love, does not mean you will have an easier time of it. With experience and knowledge, tasks can seem simpler, but that doesn't guarantee that they will be easier. You still need to exercise your effort and persistence for "continuous improvement" discussed previously in this book as the Japanese business philosophy, "Kaizen." Things may not go the way you think or even like all of the time, but what you can expect is that you will have an engaging journey as you chart your map and then travel it in the real world.

If you are not sure what you enjoy doing, it is time to get back in touch with your core self and ask deliberate questions of your unconscious mind. You want to use mindfulness as the tool to examine the pattern of activities you have enjoyed in the past.

Exercise 25: Exploring What You Love to Do

What have you noticed has been a source of enjoyment throughout your life in the nature of your:

- Hobbies?
- Topics of interest?
- Exercise?
- Eating?
- Work?
- Relationships?
- Social events?
- Holidays?
- Spiritual, Philosophical and Scientific thoughts?

If you are still not sure, it is best to start exploring the possibilities by actually giving things a try and making a decision about them later. You need to allow yourself the time to explore what may hold importance and joy for you, as only time will tell, and things take time.

If you still can't decide, then accept and get on with what you are already doing but with more effort, passion and commitment to decide whether it is for you. Maybe along the way you will fall in love with your current position or maybe you will reveal what you do actually want as you explore the opportunities around you.

Following your intuition

It is crucial that you follow your gut feeling rather than logical mind when it comes to finding your path. Often, we have great skills in an area, but they don't align to us feeling happy and positive in the moment. You may teach maths as your daytime job, but you actually prefer the mathematics of music. Every evening you enjoy playing a musical instrument with expression. You come to the realisation that maybe you should be teaching music alongside your maths or teaching and playing music exclusively.

We are allowed to make changes in our life as it is our life and we only have one of them as far as we can humanly tell. We do not have to sacrifice our own life to please others. This would be a big mistake as by serving others and not your own values, beliefs and passions is tantamount to personal self-sabotage and will likely lead to future feelings of regret, bitterness and anger.

The clutter of life

To aid in your clarity to find meaning, start to minimise the distractions in your life. By getting rid of the physical, mental and digital clutter, you can begin to focus without less worthy things pulling your attention.

If your concentration is poor and you are struggling, take on the extreme 90% rule. Rate you possessions, your hobbies, your activities and your commitments out of 10; 1 being of the lowest value and 10 being the highest. Cut out 90% of the things that rate less than 9 out of 10 in terms of their feelings of importance or function and then focus on only the 10%. If this is too harsh, try cutting 80% or 70% of the things on your ranking list.

The Buddha gave up everything but the clothes on his back. He left his life as former Prince Siddhartha Gautama who was destined to be a King in Nepal to wander and ponder the meaning of life as he travelled the lands without shelter and only the food he foraged or was donated by others. He remained happy and thoughtful in his communication with people he met along the way, despite his extreme lifestyle.

There is a whole community of modern day nomads and mini-malists whose reflections on their personal lifestyles can be found on YouTube.

Going with the flow and letting go

When life unravels in a way that doesn't meet your expectations, you feel pain and angst. When you know what is in and out of your control, you are much more resigned to manage what you can actu-ally manage. You are actually quite lucky to be able to develop the awareness that you can learn to control your attitudes and reactions with positivity.

We must all resign ourselves to the process of life; the illness, the disasters and death, as that is the reality of our physical world. How we can use that information to our advantage is to think like the Stoics of Ancient Greece did, who focused on the moment and found simple pleasure in whatever they noticed around them. It gave them more zest for life and an appreciation for the moment by accepting its beauty. This was their path to happiness. They kept death in mind every single day to remind themselves of the fleetingness of time.

Dedication to a passion, whether it be a career, belief or lifestyle brings much joy to many people. They follow their path through the ups and the downs with an overall feeling of happiness. A friend of mine is a well-known street artist in London and he can be found lying on the street pavements painting amazing scenes and portraits on chewing gum. He has been doing this for a number of years and has been interviewed on tv, film, and has had books written about his work.

Despite the glamour of the media, his artistic canvas remains the hard and often freezing cold pavement of the streets for pretty much 365 days of the year. Sometimes he is commissioned or paid for the 10 to 20% of the art that he produces, which is enough to just get by financially while he continues the other 80% of his day-to-day artistry. This 80%, he creates for free, out of his love for others and the dedication to his talents. This is the 80/20 rule in real world action. When you see him out on that pavement no matter what the weather, this is what you come to understand: what others see as an extreme sacrifice for a passion, is a labour of love for the creative soul who perceives no sacrifice, only joy.

The damage of interference

Interfering is stepping outside of your own control to impose your views and beliefs upon others. This is not a route to happiness for yourself or others. If we live such short lives on this earth, why do people want to constrain others when they are not hurting or bothering anyone? Is it jealousy, anger, resentment, or a cheap thrill perhaps?

It is because they cannot let go of control, they cannot allow their personal rules and beliefs to be broken by others. These are people who will find it impossible to live a happy and positive life as they have handed their personal control to others and the outside world.

People who have not learned to work from their own locus of control can be found everywhere, especially on online forums and discussion groups. Many of them are online "trolls" who appear angry with the world through their constrained, limited thinking and hurtful views. Often trolls will gang up together to form a like-minded group to justify their comments online. They find joy and humour in doing so at someone else's expense. However this momentary happiness is short-lived as they return to their real worlds where their emotional reactions are at the whim of external happenings. Unfortunately, as a result, they are likely to be unhappy, cynical and negative about the world, and with themselves as well. Imagine how different their lives would be if they always looked for the best in others and the world, if they could just see the positives and the opportunities around them and they took responsibility for their own actions.

Allowing energy to flow in yourself and outwardly to others

With all our learning and our practice of accepting, there is one more thing that gives meaning to our lives and brings many happy feelings, the act of giving. If we are made of energy and energy flows between us, then giving it is the process of continuing this flow. It is a continual exchange of energy, without resistance.

In acting and in particular, improvisation, a scene can only flow if there is give-and-take; that is, if you deliver a line to another actor, it must be open enough to allow the other actor to respond with an open line as well. When you deliver a line and receive a response that is very difficult to respond to, it is known as "blocking." We have all come across "blockers" in our lives, they restrict the flow of giving, they often pull positive solutions into negative dead ends. Conversation and interaction quickly comes to a halt with someone who blocks.

"THE MEANING of life is to find your gift. The purpose of life is to give it away."
Pablo Picasso

THERE IS nothing you can achieve or buy that will make you happy for ever. It is best to choose happiness first and align your life with this choice. This means fending off all the obstacles and restrictions and deliberate attempts to pull you into negativity, including your own doubts. You must like who you are and know that all your reactions, responses and attitudes come from your locus of control. Nobody else can make you be happy and only a person with their own issues with happiness would try to make you unhappy. Your purpose in life is to consistently operate from your personal self-esteem and control.

HAPPINESS IS an experience that comes from the inside, not an item to possess, nor give. You can however create an environment conducive to happiness from all that you say and do, where positive and happy energy flows. The following external factors will not ensure your happiness:

- Relying on external rewards as the moments won't last.
- Buying and possessing, as the initial high quickly subsides and the possession will wear out, become unfashionable or be lost, stolen or damaged.
- Physical and sensory highs, as they will pass, or you will become desensitised to the effect of them if you indulge too much.

HAPPINESS IS MADE up of positive moments and small pleasures which are sustainable. The Ancient Greeks followed the known expression,

"NOTHING IN EXCESS and everything in moderation."

IF YOU PURSUE difficult to attain moments and achievements as your only source of happiness, you will not be happy very often. Happiness first and then everything else after. Happiness may be a short-term by-product of achieving something big, but a long-term by-product of choosing to be happy now, means you may well achieve more and achieve more often.

"SUCCESS IS NOT the key to happiness. Happiness is the key to success."
Albert Schweitzer

WHEN YOU FEEL yourself being challenged by negative or unhappy feelings, ask:

- "What one positive thing can I see in this or learn from this?"

Or, if the challenge is overwhelming:

- "What is the silver lining in this dark cloud?"

"WHAT IS the meaning of life? To be happy and useful."
The Dalai Lama

13

IN CONCLUSION
CONTINUING A HAPPY LIFE

The purpose of this book has been to guide your thinking toward the positive habit of maintaining optimistic thoughts and actions. It is through this practice that we will be happy more often. There is no one and nothing that will help you to be happy until you are consistently asserting your own power of choice. When you exercise your personal positive choice, you will no longer feel swayed or tempted to lose out to the negativity from others, or from yourself.

WHENEVER YOU CATCH A NEGATIVE THOUGHT, stop, breathe in, smile and say to yourself,

"I AM BETTER THAN THIS."

The 10 rules of happiness

If you strip away all the detail, "Happy more often" can be summarised in these 10 practices:

1. I am in control of my own reactions, choices and attitudes.
2. I can only inspire change for the outside world by behaving as the role-model for that change I wish to see.
3. I accept and let go of what I cannot control, including comparing myself to others or pleasing them.
4. I forgive myself for past mistakes and I forgive others for their mistakes too.
5. I take notice of and appreciate the small things in life and I'm grateful for their existence.
6. I am mindful of the moment and consciously live in the now as much as possible.
7. I don't wait to attain good feelings, as they are not attainable. I can experience them right now by changing my mindset.
8. Fear is simply an imagined negative perception of the future that has not yet happened to me.
9. I have choices to make all day long, so I choose happiness, optimism and positivity in all situations, as any negative choice would pull me down.
10. The meaning of life is learning what my gift is and giving it to the world.

YOU HOLD a lot of potential power in the strengths that make up your personality. Choose to act on these strengths alone with effort and persistence.

Realise that what holds you back in life is putting too much credence in what others tell you to do and not do, and the doubts that follow. No entrepreneur or self-starter in life has faed an easy ride. They have continually faced criticism from loved ones and strangers. It has been their belief in themselves and what they have to offer that has helped them weather every storm they have encountered. Their beliefs in their personal strengths have been the source of their happiness.

A very young child believes they can create anything in their world which starts in their imagination and is then enacted in their role-play. As an adult, choose a positive role that brings you more happiness and success and impacts the world in a good way.

THERE IS an ancient Chinese proverb that states,

"BETTER TO LIGHT **a candle than curse the darkness.**"

I THANK you for your commitment to reading "Happy more often" and I wish you a happy and successful life.

ABOUT THE AUTHOR

Andrew-John Paterson resides in London, England, and works as a school management consultant and author of books and articles on school leadership and personal self-development. Andrew has taught in and led a number of Government and Private schools as a teacher and Headteacher.

After studying counselling, Andrew was fascinated by the power of the unconscious mind and went on to study at the London School of Clinical Hypnosis and then Neuro-Linguistic Programming with Richard Bandler and Paul McKenna. Andrew has developed a passion for using language to help others change their lives.

You can find out more by visiting: miniteaching.com

OTHER BOOKS BY A-J PATERSON

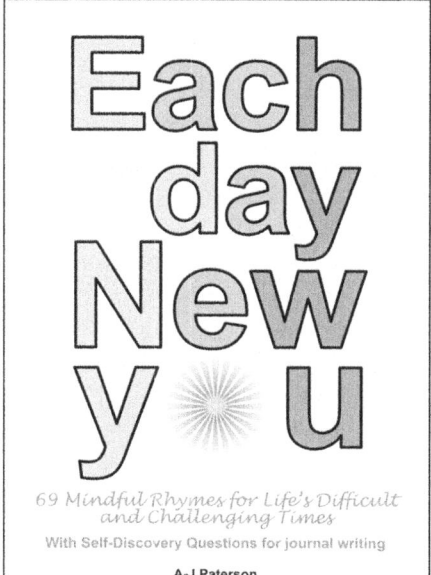

Each day New you

69 Mindful Rhymes for Life's Difficult
and Challenging Times

With Self-Discovery Questions for journal writing

A-J Paterson

mindful

minimalism

The What, the Why and the How

of decluttering, and

Living with Less

A-J Paterson

Made in the USA
Monee, IL
13 March 2023

29681171R10125